PETER RIDD

AND THE CASE FOR ACADEMIC FREEDOM

Edited by Morgan Begg

Connor Court Publishing

PETER RIDD AND THE CASE FOR ACADEMIC FREEDOM

First published in 2023 by the Institute of Public Affairs,
Level 2, 410 Collins Street, Melbourne, Victoria, 3000
Phone: 03 9600 4744
www.ipa.org.au

This edition published by Connor Court Publishing, 2024

Connor Court Publishing, PO BOX 7257, Redland Bay, QLD, 4165

Copyright © the Institute of Public Affairs 2023, 2024

All rights reserved

ISBN: 9781923224407

Cover photograph/illustration: Dimitri Mathieu
Cover design and typeset by Krisztina Strzebonski
Printed in Australia

Contents

___

Introduction

Morgan Begg

—

Academic freedom is in a state of crisis in Australia.

For decades universities have been dominated by left wing political thought and affiliation, but even so they were once seen as a place where debate could take place, and that this would even be fostered by academic staff. This is no longer the case. Our universities have become increasingly dogmatic: students censor other students, academics censor other academics, and university administrators have no regard for academic freedom at all.

One only need consider the response to Bjorn Lomborg attempting to launch at the University of Western Australia a research centre modelled on Bjorn Lomborg's Copenhagan Consensus Centre. Lomborg achieved fame as *The Sceptical Environmentalist*, who argues that the costs of policies aimed at mitigating climate change far outweigh the benefits. The centre was aimed at developing peer-reviewed research to help inform policy, the same way that numerous other research centres in academia do. Academics campaigned against it, and the plans to establish the research centre were dropped.

Another prominent example took place in the humanities. The Ramsay Centre for Western Civilisation was established in 2017 through an endowment by Paul Ramsay, a prominent Australian businessman and philanthropist. Ramsay wanted to ensure young Australians were given the opportunity to learn about the extraordinary gifts Australia has received as a descendent of Western Civilisation. It took years for the centre to launch properly because on numerous occasions, its attempts to partner with universities to offer its programme were cancelled due to staff uproar. Even today a website for "Staff against the Ramsay Centre" remains active, featuring an open letter by University of Sydney staff calling on the university to reject the Ramsay Centre, on the basis that the staff supported "academic autonomy and diversity".

These actions are being felt by students too. As early as 2019, research by the Institute of Public Affairs revealed how university students felt the shadow of cancel culture. At the time, 41 per cent of students sometimes felt unable to express their opinions, 31 per cent had been made to feel uncomfortable by a teacher for their views, and 59 per cent believed they were sometimes prevented from voicing their opinions on contentious issues by other students.

Academic freedom needed a champion – and that's when Peter Ridd stepped up. As he will explain in his own words in the following pages (Chapter 1), Peter had become deeply concerned about what was happening in the scientific profession. He had become aware of the replication crisis in the sciences, where a concerningly high number of findings were the result of research which was not able to be repeated. Science was becoming less rigorous, including in his area of expertise, the Great Barrier Reef (GBR).

Since 1989 Peter had been a professor of physics at James Cook University, and as a long-standing member of academia had experienced what it was like to work in an environment where debate and inquiry was somewhat allowed. He not unreasonably expected to be able to talk about the problems in reef science. But Peter would soon learn just how much universities had changed with respect to academic freedom, when he emailed a journalist to call to attention unreliable research about the supposed decline of the reef in late 2015.

Peter was soon issued with an official censure by JCU who argued that criticising the research produced by organisations connected to the university amounted to failures to be collegiate and to uphold the reputation of the university. Despite the direction to be silent in the future, Peter rightly felt this was incompatible with his role as a scientist, being one who rejects dogma in favour of rigorous scepticism.

Unfortunately, the school of thought that Peter represents has in recent years become unfashionable. If one statement could sum up the problem in science it would be this assertion by Hans-Otto Pörtner, from the Alfred Wegener Institute in Germany, who claimed that a scientist "building a career on judging what other people did is not right… if such a controversy gets outside of the community, it's harmful because the whole community loses credibility."

It almost goes without saying that Pörtner is a deeply entrenched figure in the so-called climate sciences, a field of science significantly resistant to critique or challenge. In fact, Pörtner is a co-chair of the United Nations' Intergovernmental Panel on Climate Change whose purpose is to further the notion of anthropogenic climate change.

Science isn't a community because there isn't really a commonality of interests among all scientists. Science is, or ought to be, a hyper-competitive environment where hypotheses are diligently tested and research is challenged in the pursuit of improving society's knowledge of the world.

It may be more accurate to interpret Pörtner as not referring to a community, but to the institution of The Science. The Science is not the profession or practice of science, but how the profession is manipulated in order to generate particular policy goals – such as forcing Western governments to sign onto plans to change its energy sources. This is why Peter Ridd's case is so important.

If Ridd was challenging the quality of scientific research conducted by organisations associated with his university for his own gratification, to prove he is right and that others are wrong, this would be no less deserving of academic freedom protections. But that is not all Ridd was doing: he was challenging the scientific basis upon which a great deal of public policy is based. Environmental activism and policy in Australia is often justified on the basis that the GBR is dying. So when Ridd challenges the assumptions about the death of the GBR, this is in fact a significant threat to an ecosystem of powerful interests who depend on the idea of a dying reef.

It is telling that at no point did JCU ever attempt to prove Ridd was wrong in what he was saying. Indeed, Ridd has actually been proven right over time. It was only in January 2022 that "factcheckers" at the AAP attempted to challenge the assertions about the GBR put forward by Ridd (one of the few to attempt this, it seems). In a Facebook post, Ridd claimed that the GBR did not need help because the major regions of the reef "never had more coral on them." When contacted by the AAP, Ridd said this was based on Australian Institute of Marine Science (AIMS) long term monitoring data on coral cover of three sections of the reef, adding that it was "absolutely beyond doubt" there had never been more coral on the reef since records began. The AAP said at the time that Ridd was mostly false, citing as evidence those who Ridd had criticised in the past for putting forward unreliable science.

Fast forward to August 2022, when *The Australian* reported on a survey by the AIMS long term monitoring data, which found that the GBR had set a new record for hard coral cover over two-third of its 2,300 kilometre length. In other words, Dr Ridd was completely vindicated yet again. It goes without saying that the AAP Factcheck showing Ridd was "mostly false" has not been updated.

Before all this though, Peter suffered through years of disciplinary measures from his former employer, culminating in his dismissal from his post in May 2018. But prior to this, Peter had already recognised that this dispute could only be resolved in the courts. Peter's actions were ostensibly protected in his employment contract, or enterprise agreement, as an exercise of the right of intellectual freedom. A separate clause of the enterprise agreement even provided that the Code of Conduct, that the university relied on to censure and punish Peter, could not detract from the right to intellectual freedom. Since the university never gave any regard to this, it would be up to the courts to enforce the contract. After decisions in the Federal Circuit Court and the Full Court of the Federal Court, the High Court finally handed down the final decision on 13 October 2021.

The High Court, by unanimous decision, made some positive comments about academic freedom, but did not apply them to Peter's case. That the High Court was unable to back in academic freedom, when it was expressly protected by the employment contract was a disappointment to put it lightly. But it was in reading the court's decision that the multitude of errors and misconstructions became apparent.

The JCU narrative was quickly adopted and shared in the media. "Oh yes the High Court endorsed academic freedom, but Ridd wasn't sacked for that, it was because of the confidentiality orders." Even some of the country's most reliable voices for freedom, such as Janet Albrechtsen and Henry Ergas, wrote in columns in *The Australian* that the court's decision was the right one, and even commending the court for what it said about academic freedom.

My view at the time was simple: what the High Court said about academic freedom was worthless because it had no bearing on the actual outcome of the case. It was dead letter. A cynic could be forgiven for thinking that these comments were added by the court in order to provide cover for their actual decision to endorse JCUs actions in sacking Peter.

Because of this, the IPA thought it was important to provide a proper analysis explaining not only why JCU was wrong to dismiss Peter, but why the High Court was wrong to endorse JCU's actions. We convened a Symposium for academic freedom, held in Noosa on 13 May 2022. Everybody in attendance participated in the Symposium but a smaller number led the discussion, and following the event I asked for submissions to be collected for publication.

Peter Ridd provides his personal observations of his tortuous quest for justice inside and out of Australia's legal system, framed by an exploration of his extensive background in GBR research, including how he first became aware, and then deeply concerned, about the significant shortcomings in the quality of scientific research.

In my chapter, I untangle the High Court's confused judgement, explaining the various failures in reasoning underlying the decision. I argue that Peter's case shows there is no easy fix for academic freedom because the courts and the university administrators will frustrate it unless serious and substantial reform to the university sector takes place.

A more optimisitic view was given by **Chris Merritt**, the Vice President of the Rule of Law Institute of Australia, who argued that the High Court's rhetorical endorsement of academic freedom was another sign of the momentum shifting in favour of freedom of speech on campus. As Chris argues, it just remains for the politicians to seize the initiative.

James Allan, the Garrick Professor of Law at the University of Queensland, explores how top-down, politically biased grant obsessed universities have harmed freedom of speech on campus, and concludes by excoriating the High Court's decision which, in his words, has enervated the entire concept of academic freedom itself.

And the final chapter is by **Aynsley Kellow**, the emeritus professor of government at the University of Tasmania, who covers the serious and proven problems that have been uncovered in the sciences. He notes that the High Court's rejection of Peter's case is not just the endpoint of a cascade of injustice against Peter, but against the basic principles of scientific endeavour and thereby the public who depend on high-quality science to inform public policy.

In an ideal world, Peter would be employed in a university without controversy, producing high quality and rigorous research with a right to speak out about the reef. Unfortunately, this is not the world we live in, but it is a small consolation that following the High Court's decision, Peter agreed to work as a fellow at the Institute of Public Affairs, leading our work on the "Project for Real Science". This initiative will rebuild the integrity of scientific research in Australia, with a special focus on the Great Barrier Reef. It has been my pleasure to have the opportunity to support Peter's fight for freedom of speech on climate science, and to assist him now in a most important mission to save science in Australia. I hope you enjoy the following chapters, as I have enjoyed collecting them and thereby helping correct the record on Peter Ridd's case for academic freedom.

Background
and observations

Peter Ridd

—

In order to put *Ridd v James Cook University*[1] into context, it is useful to consider the background and detailed sequence of events that led to the legal action. At the time I was fired in 2018, I was Professor of Physics at James Cook University (JCU) and had built a research career since 1984 working on a wide range of topics including the physical oceanography of the Great Barrier Reef (GBR), physical processes in mangrove swamps, electromagnetic geophysical prospecting methods, instrumentation development, weed killing robots, and quality assurance (QA) of scientific research. I had published more than 100 scientific publications. In addition, I led a university-owned consultancy operation working mostly on port dredge environmental monitoring, and instrumentation to support the mining industry.[2]

My research on the GBR and QA systems in science ultimately led to conflict with JCU. By 2015, it became clear that, contrary to the conventional wisdom, the GBR was in a healthy condition, and that there were fundamental problems with the QA systems in reef-science institutions that were giving wrong, or misleading, information about the reef.

One of the reasons I came to this conclusion is that I had an unusual background for a marine scientist, most of whom are biologists. By contrast my undergraduate degree from JCU (1978-80) was in physics and maths, with a smattering of geology. In addition, my industry work had made me familiar with formal QA systems. Most scientists have such little experience with QA systems that they do not even know they are ignorant of them.

My career began as a teacher at Blackheath and Thornburgh College in Charters Towers; then in 1984 I was employed at the Australian Institute of Marine Science (AIMS) as a scientist. I was contributing to research into the physical oceanography of the GBR, working on tides, ocean currents, waves, and movement of sediment, all of which are crucial to understand its biology. I also worked in the in the estuaries of the Gulf of Carpentaria and Northern Territory, in mangrove swamps, and developing instrumentation to measure a range of environmental parameters. At the same time as working at AIMS, I was studying part-time for my PhD in physics, modelling and experimenting with antennas for use in geophysical prospecting.

In 1989, I commenced a postdoctoral fellowship at the newly formed Marine Geophysical Laboratory (MGL) at JCU, with which I was associated until I was fired. The MGL was a collaboration between the physics and geology departments at JCU and was heavily involved with research into the geological history and physical processes of the GBR. One of the founding professors was Professor Bob Carter who later become one of the world's most prominent opponents of climate alarmism.

Working with geologists gave me a very different perspective, compared with biologists, when considering changes to ecosystems such as the GBR. The geologists of the MGL had documented the monumental changes occurring on the GBR over the last few thousand years – the massive changes in sea level, the formation of new reefs, and the destruction of others. Whereas a biologist might view a change to a reef as most likely the result of human activity, a geologist will often ask if those changes are in line with what has occurred in the past.

Much of my work in the 1990s was with Dr Piers Larcombe, a sedimentologist. We worked on the coral reefs close to the coast that are often affected by high mud concentrations. Biologists often stated that the "inshore" coral reefs had been adversely affected by soil erosion from farms washing down rivers onto the reefs, and by dredging of mud in ports. My main contribution was co-inventing the first instruments that could take measurements of sediment concentrations in coastal waters for long periods.

Using our instrumentation, Larcombe and Dr Ken Woolfe showed that the inshore reefs of the Queensland coast were highly turbid (muddy) well before European settlement and that the impact of farming and dredging was minimal. Larcombe and Woolfe used drill-cores of the inshore reefs to document the history of these reefs – they had always been murky, muddy reefs. This was a controversial result that was largely ignored by the dominant groups in the marine science community. Larcombe, Woolfe, and I were arguing there was minimal impact of anthropogenic sediment on the GBR.

At the time I was fired, my group had taken more measurements of sediment concentrations around the GBR than all the other groups combined, but our work was routinely ignored in major official scientific documents, such as the *2017 Scientific Consensus Statement*.[3]

1998 was a pivotal year for the debate on climate change and the future of the GBR. This was when the alarmism about climate morphed from a debatable hypothesis to an immutable, incontestable "fact". A major El Niño event, and the hot water associated with it, had caused major bleaching of the GBR. It made headlines as proof that "climate change was real" and that the reef was in mortal peril. At that time I was on the alarmist side of the climate change argument, however, I felt that the data on the 1998 bleaching event, and a follow-up event in 2002, was being misused to push a fallacious argument about the reef and climate change. It was becoming apparent to me that my own work on sediment was not the only area where ideology was trumping hard evidence.

From the early 2000s, a considerable number of high-profile papers started to be written supposedly showing the demise of the reef. These were often quoted in the mainstream media. Examples were papers supposedly showing the reef was 28 per cent down the path to ecological extinction; had suffered a precipitate fall in growth rates since the 1990s; and had suffered a halving of coral cover since the 1960s. With co-workers I responded to these by writing a series of papers demonstrating that there were serious flaws in this alarmist research.[4]

What was most concerning was not that the original flawed papers had passed the peer-review process; it was the difficulty that I found in getting the corrections published. The original journals routinely refused to publish our commentary; I was forced to publish in alternative journals, such as the *Indian Journal of Marine Science* (a very good journal, but it is unconventional to publish corrections in a different journal to the original article). I was coming to the conclusion that groupthink was becoming deeply entrenched and that alternative views were being silenced by the journals' peer-review process.

Parallel to my efforts to critique the conventional doom-science about the reef, my funding from the Australian Research Council

(ARC) dried up in 2007. Until then I had received a steady stream of funding from the ARC, but I started to get peer reviews of funding applications that suggested my views were unacceptable, and this was a reason to not fund the proposed research project.

The replication crisis: a horrible revelation

In 2013, my brother, also a scientist, sent me an article from *The Economist* magazine documenting huge problems in biomedical sciences with "replication," which described how scientists are very often unable to reproduce the work of other scientists.[5] This failure of replication applied especially to high-profile "quality" journals authored by scientists from prestigious universities. I read more widely and came across the work of John Ioannidis who had blown the whistle on what had become known as the "replication crisis". Ioannidis had published a highly cited paper, entitled, "Why most published research findings are false".[6] This work was making waves across the scientific community.

As a scientist for most of my career, I found this deeply concerning. I questioned if there were any other professions so unreliable as science. Half is wrong! And we have been told that scientists must be believed – "follow the Science."

I literally became depressed. I had prided myself on being a member of a noble profession, but the evidence was indicating that used car salesmen and politicians were more trustworthy.

Until about 2002, I had thought that the scientific community was unreliable in my own field of expertise – sediments around coral reefs – but I presumed that the rest of the GBR science must be solid. By 2012, I was convinced that GBR science was full of flaws, but presumed this was a problem particular to the environmental sciences where ideology can easily creep in. Surely the rest of published science was solid. But, no. It is now well accepted that a huge percentage of recently published peer-reviewed work in virtually all areas of science is wrong.

It now became apparent to me that there was a systemic problem with QA processes in science. It relied on the peer-review system, which was patently inadequate. The general public thinks that the peer review of a scientific paper is done by a group of maybe a dozen scientists who take months checking the work and repeating experiments. In reality it is often just a quick read of the work, for maybe just a few hours, by a couple of other scientists. It is far short of a decent QA process.

Until 2013, I had spent considerable time trying to correct flawed work about the GBR. But in QA systems, the most important aspect is not just correcting the flaw, it is asking what caused the flaw in the first place so that it can be prevented on other occasions. I came to the conclusion that it was essential to focus on the obvious and well documented weaknesses in the science QA systems, not the detail of the scientific flaws. This is how industry approaches such problems.

To this end I started working on two major projects, both with Larcombe: a review report on the sedimentology of the GBR;[7] and a paper on the implications of the replication crisis to GBR research.[8] Both had a focus on QA systems.

Battle lines drawn

By 2015, it was apparent that my views on the GBR were becoming a problem for JCU. My superior had told me that informal complaints had been made. In addition, Professor Bob Carter, who was then a very well-known climate sceptic, had been pushed out of JCU because his views were not acceptable. I started predicting that it was most likely that I would not leave JCU of my own volition.

In late 2015, I became interested in a set of pictures of the coral reef at Stone Island that supposedly showed the reef in the 1890s with lush coral, and then more recent pictures showing a barren wasteland. The pictures were being used by many organisations, including the Great Barrier Reef Marine Park Authority (GBRMPA) and JCU's Australian Centre of Excellence for Coral Reef Studies (CECRS) to supposedly show that all the inshore reefs of the GBR were impacted by farm run-off. I decided to despatch a couple of field technicians to check the surprising proposition that there was no coral around Stone Island. They found and photographed a large amount of very heathy coral disproving the notion that there had been a major change since the 1890s.

My concern was not that an error had been made (which was obvious). It was about the QA failure that had occurred. What systems were in place at GBRMPA and CECRS to check these conclusions? What other results were affected by this QA failure and how could this be avoided in the future?

A few weeks after the abundant heathy coral was found near Stone Island, a journalist from the *Courier-Mail* contacted me about another issue. I alerted the journalist to the new information on the Stone Island reefs and posed a series of questions he might ask GBRMPA and the CECRS. Professor Hughes of the CECRS filed an official complaint against me to JCU.

I was charged with "misconduct", subjected to a disciplinary process, and instructed to remain silent about the entire process – a confidentiality order. I was found guilty of breaking the JCU "Code of Conduct" and warned that a future transgression could result in dismissal. I was officially censured.

This was profoundly upsetting. I had demonstrated that an important scientific result that was being used to guide government management and legislation was completely wrong. I had endeavoured to be as polite as possible when pointing out this error, but, as I stated in our defence to JCU, it is very difficult to identify a serious quality problem with others' work without somebody getting upset.

It was now clearly only a matter of time before JCU would remove me unless I completely stopped arguing about the QA issue in reef science.

Beginning of the end

In mid-2017, I published a chapter in an Institute of Public Affairs (IPA) book *Climate Change: The Facts 2017* edited by Jennifer Marohasy. In this chapter I argued that the reef was in good shape and that the replication crisis, which was well accepted in many other areas of science, was seriously affecting reef science. I was contacted by Alan Jones, a well-known media personality in Australia, to do an interview about the chapter. In that interview I stated that, due to systemic QA failings, much of the work coming from reef-science organisations was not trustworthy. I also stated that many scientists were understandably emotionally attached to the reef, which affected their judgement. At the end of the interview I was completely unaware that it was going to cause a big problem.

A few days later, I was contacted by the Dean of JCU to arrange a time to meet, as there was apparently a serious issue with the interview. I guessed I would again be charged with misconduct and would be placed under confidentiality directions. I knew it was essential to make it well-known that something was happening before I was issued with any allegations that would greatly restrict what I could publicly say in my defence. I contacted Jennifer Marohasy and told her I knew no details but that the future was not looking good.

On 21 August 2017, I was issued allegations that I had broken the code of conduct, and that this might constitute "serious misconduct". Although the confidentiality clauses of the enterprise agreement were very ambiguous, it was now risky to talk about any detail of the allegations; however, because I had already contacted Jennifer Marohasy, I was able to talk about the existence of the allegations because these were in the public domain *before* I was charged.

Due largely to Jennifer Marohasy and the Institute of Public Affairs (IPA), the story was heavily reported in the media, particularly by Graham Lloyd from *The Australian*.[9] I started to receive a lot of emails from friends, staff, and students concerning my predicament. I did not reveal any details of the charges at that time. In one paragraph of an email, which was ultimately used against me by JCU, I even defended JCU stating:

> I should say that despite what is happening now, JCU is not worse than other universities – in fact I always say that it is a bit special because I have lasted much longer than I would have done if I was at UQ. In my view our whole university system pretends to value free debate, but in fact it crushes it whenever the "wrong" ideas are spoken. They are truly an Orwellian in nature.

By this stage JCU was reading all my emails. On 23 October, JCU issued roughly 25 new allegations of serious misconduct based on these emails. I had never sweated so much in my life as when I realised JCU was trawling through every word I was writing. What had I said in an unguarded moment? I was pleased, and mildly surprised, after reading all the allegations (which covered about

80 pages) that there was nothing about which I was ashamed. It was clear this was a fishing expedition to instil fear – and it worked.

It became obvious that legal action was going to be needed and papers were prepared accordingly to file in court. This was done on 20 November. I had contacted Graham Lloyd from *The Australian* with all the information that was filed. A long article reporting the case in great detail was published in *The Australian*.[10]

The next day JCU, perhaps surprised by events and the publicity, issued a "final censure" against me. I had not been fired but had been put on a very short leash. Any minor transgression could now be used as an excuse for termination. It would be effectively impossible to continue to make the argument that QA systems of other scientists or organisations were deficient as that would contravene the code of conduct. I had escaped termination but was effectively muzzled.

The reality of this muzzling became apparent in late November 2017 when I was invited to give two public lectures: one for the IPA and the other at the Sydney Institute. I was instructed to submit my presentations to the Dean for vetting and suggestions were made to remove various slides. I was prevented from making the case that there were systemic QA problems with GBR science.

After lengthy consideration, my wife Cheryl and I thought there was no choice but to continue with the legal action. I could not remain silent, and termination was inevitable unless a successful legal challenge could be made.

Raising funds for the legal challenge

Inevitably the biggest problem with legal action is the cost. It was initially estimated that a court case would cost around $100,000. It was decided to try crowdfunding – a very risky proposition. Worse, for people to feel confident enough to donate, *all* the details of the allegations against me needed to be made public. Donors had to be sure there was nothing sinister about my actions, that I had not been censured for laziness or sexual impropriety or the like. But releasing and publicising all the information would break JCU's dubious confidentiality direction. Crowdfunding was thus a very high-risk strategy, with no guarantee that donors would come forth. The publicity would not please JCU, and the confidentiality order would have to be challenged legally.

It was decided to wait until after Christmas 2017 to launch the GoFundMe campaign. A web page with all the relevant information was built and the crowdfunding went live on 31 January. In just 49 hours we raised $95,000 – an incredible result. People were scandalised by JCU's actions and wanted to help. I suspect that people have seen too much of this cancel culture at universities and were itching for the opportunity to contribute to the fight.

By the time the High Court proceedings came to an end in October 2021, a total of $1.5 million had been donated by more than 10,000 people in two major GoFundMe campaigns. This was in addition to $300,000 that we spent from our own resources. This allowed a very powerful team of lawyers to be engaged, led by Stuart Wood KC AM, ably assisted by Mitchell Downes, Ben Jellis, Ben Kidston, Amelia Hasson and others. Without this brilliant team, far less would have been achieved.

JCU continues to smash its own reputation

JCU's response to the GoFundMe campaign and the media attention that followed was predictable. They started the process of termination. New allegations were found including my favourite, the "no satire" directive. I had sent a copy of a newspaper article about the case to an ex-colleague and friend in France. Despite not mentioning any detail about the case, JCU charged me with satirising the disciplinary process by writing "for your amusement" in the subject line of the email. This "no satire" directive was derided in the media.[11]

The legal proceedings

I am aware that I am emotionally too close to the case and have too little legal knowledge to be able to make a detailed analysis of the legal arguments; however, I will make the following observations.

In the end the case came down to an interpretation of JCU's Enterprise Agreement (enterprise agreement). There was a clash between the code of conduct, which required me to be polite and uphold the reputation of the university, and the enterprise agreement's clauses on "intellectual freedom". The intellectual freedom clauses allow robust debate and also allowed staff to express disagreement with university decisions and processes.

Important lines from these clauses (written out in full in the Appendix) are:

13.3.   The parties note that the Code of Conduct is not intended to detract from Clause 14, *Intellectual Freedom*

14.1.   JCU is committed to act in a manner consistent with the protection and promotion of intellectual freedom within the University and in accordance with JCU's Code of Conduct.

14.2.   Intellectual freedom includes the rights of staff to:

• Participate in public debate and express opinions about issues and ideas related to their respective fields of competence;

- Express opinions about the operations of JCU and higher education policy more generally;

14.4.   JCU acknowledges the rights of staff to express disagreement with University decisions and with the processes used to make those decisions.

The code of conduct contains language that contradicts the intellectual freedom clauses and thus the main legal argument was about which was superior. If the code of conduct prevailed, I did not dispute that I would lose – in this sense it was an all-or-nothing argument. However, if the intellectual freedom clauses prevailed, then, provided it was determined that I was exercising that right, I should win.

In addition, there was a clause covering confidentiality, which JCU was also using to argue that it could silence me.

The case was heard by three courts; the difference in judgements is remarkable. At the Federal Circuit Court, Justice Vasta ruled that intellectual freedom prevailed over the code of conduct and that the confidentiality clause "is there for the protection of the staff member" to prevent the university releasing details of their allegations to the public without the staff member's permission.

At appeal in the Federal Court, a majority decision overruled the decision of the lower court and found that the code of conduct prevailed over intellectual freedom. The majority also ruled that the confidentiality clause allowed JCU to silence me about the disciplinary process. The dissenting judge, Justice Rangiah, disagreed and also commented on the "Kafkaesque" nature of the confidentiality rulings.

The High Court agreed with me, Justice Vasta, and Justice Rangiah on the main points of construction – that intellectual freedom prevailed over the code of conduct – and that the university had unlawfully censured me. However, it also ruled that the university had the right to enforce confidentiality about the entire proceedings and was justified in firing me on these grounds. They also ruled that some of the statements I made were not within my field of expertise and thus not covered by intellectual freedom. An example given in the judgement was my assertion that "our whole university system pretends to value free debate, but in fact is crushes it".[12]

We thus won the main argument on whether the code of conduct was subservient to academic freedom but lost because I spoke about JCU's unlawful activity.

Others are more qualified to talk about the legal details, but some aspects of the decision seem remarkable. First, the High Court decision does not explain why Clause 14.4, which gives express permission for an academic to express disagreement with the university, cannot be invoked to protect him or her from the confidentiality provisions. Second, we argued that the well-known and accepted legal principle that "there is no confidence as to the disclosure of an iniquity" needed to be considered. The High Court effectively ruled that JCU was able to tell its staff members to keep its unlawful activity quiet – breaking this principle. This is a remarkable situation and JCU received no sanction whatsoever for acting unlawfully.

Nevertheless, despite the loss on a technicality, the legal standing of academic freedom has been resolved for the first time in the High Court, and the judges ruled that it is not over-ridden by codes of conduct limiting speech and debate.

This is a major step forward.

Background debate

The legal proceedings sparked considerable public interest about both the principle of academic freedom and QA systems in science.

In 2020, Timothy Clarke from Deakin University, and six international collaborators published a replication study[13] of work originally published by the CECRS – the organisation that I had said on Alan Jones's program lacked QA and was untrustworthy. Clarke's work attempted to verify the original findings, and their work was reported in the prestigious magazine *Science*.[14] Clarke showed that roughly a dozen of the CECRS's major reports could not be replicated or had serious flaws. This was further proof that my original comments about poor QA processes, that precipitated the legal action, were correct. This was, unfortunately, irrelevant to the legal argument.

In addition, media attention on both sides of politics were focused on problems of academic freedom at universities. *The Guardian* carried an in-depth article supporting my right to freedom of speech[15] – as did *The Australian*, the ABC and Sky News. The National Tertiary Education Union (NTEU), of which I had been a member for decades, supported my legal argument. It was thus remarkable that the IPA, which often disagrees with unions, and the NTEU were arguing on the same side against JCU. JCU, by its actions, had managed the incredible feat of uniting opposites, such as *The Guardian* and Andrew Bolt; the NTEU and the IPA.

While the case progressed through the courts, Queensland Senator Pauline Hanson, with the Coalition government, made a concerted effort to change the definitions of academic freedom in the *Higher Education Support Act 2003* to better protect academics. These amendments were passed in March 2021. If these had been in place in 2017, it is highly likely they would have afforded considerable protection, which would have prevented JCU's actions.

However, the legislation is in many regards a toothless tiger. There is no effective policing of academic freedom, and no significant fines against an errant university. The Tertiary Education Quality and Standard Agency (TEQSA), which is responsible for making sure Australian universities maintain high standards, specifically states it may take action against a university if there is a "serious risk to … [the] reputation of the higher education sector".[16] However, despite being determined by the highest court in the land that JCU had acted unlawfully, it appears that TEQSA has done nothing.

The way forward

Although the High Court decision, and the supporting amendments to the *Higher Education Support Act 2003* have placed academic freedom on a much firmer legal footing, the reality for an academic considering saying something controversial is not encouraging.

One problem is that both the High Court decision and the 2021 legislative changes concerning academic freedom require the protected speech to be "related to their respective fields of competence". This may at first appear reasonable, but such phrases are poorly defined and any doubt always works in favour of the university. Doubt favours the one with the deepest pockets. Universities have considerable financial power and ability to take the matter to an expensive legal hearing.

An example of how the field of competence limitation doubt could play badly for an academic can be found in this case. My statement that universities are Orwellian was deemed by the High Court to be outside my area of expertise. It could be argued that any academic is qualified to state such an opinion, but clearly the High Court defined field of expertise very narrowly. It could also be added that Clause 14.2 states clearly that I was permitted to express opinions about "higher education policy more generally", and thus my comments were fully covered by academic freedom.

Another example of how the "field of competence" limitation is a serious problem can be found in many other statements that I have made over the years. The question is: where is the border of one's expertise? My comments on the effect of sediment on corals would definitely be inside my competence, and my views on the QA systems in science are probably covered. But if I went further and said, as I frequently do, that government legislation based on poorly quality assured reef science means that the legislation is likely badly flawed – is that in my field of expertise and covered by academic freedom? I am not an expert on governance and legislation. It could be argued I was arguing outside my field of expertise, even though the statement is merely a corollary of the conclusions about the veracity of the science.

A much better approach to academic freedom would be to allow any speech not proscribed by law. If it can be said outside a university, why can't it be allowed inside the university.

Another problem is that the High Court have effectively ruled that a university can impose confidentiality restrictions on a disciplinary process that overrule the academic's right to academic freedom *viz.* the academic's right to express disagreement with a process of the university. In practice this gives the university great power. Being forced to remain silent about the disciplinary action is extremely intimidating. The ability to talk and seek help is taken away from the academic unless he or she is a member of a union. The academic is isolated and fearful. Confidentiality directions must be viewed as a powerful weapon wielded by the university. In my case, where legal action was required, only by making all the charges public in an easily readable form (redacting the names of third parties) was I able to raise funds for my defence.

An unrelated problem discouraging free speech at universities is the fundamental change that has occurred in almost every western university over the last couple of decades. A corporate culture has developed where the reputation of the university is much more important than the pursuit of truth. Universities are huge institutions with vast financial turnover. A university may wish to keep quiet about a scandal involving poor QA of science or other deficiencies, which should be called out by other academics. The truth is a benefit to the rest of society but not necessarily to the university; it might affect student enrolments and the flow of money.

A further problem is that university academics are now almost entirely from the political Left or hard-Left. They are generally unsympathetic and intolerant of conservative, or opposing views. They rarely find themselves in a position that their academic freedom is infringed.

There is, however, one simple thing that could be done to even up the power imbalance on academic freedom between an academic and a university. The Chancellor of the university must be made personally financially responsible if his or her university fails to maintain academic freedom. This is a similar situation that company directors are in if their company trades while insolvent or breaks major safety rules. At present there is no significant fine if a university crushes academic freedom. Even if I had won, the university would have only had to pay about $1 million, and the fine was a small fraction of that. JCU's legal expenses were probably twice that figure so this is not an incentive to uphold academic freedom.

But if the Chancellor could personally be fined $1 million, as can happen to company directors, then he or she would take the issue very seriously. The universities' financial power to take the matter to court is then largely balanced – the Chancellor would be very keen to make sure the matter was resolved properly and not risk an adverse finding that their university had broken its obligation, now written into the *Higher Education Support Act 2003*, to academic freedom of speech.

If there is only one thing that should be done, making Chancellor's personally liable is my major recommendation.

A final personal note

One thing that I have noticed over the period of this legal action, when my mind was focused on freedom of speech issues, is that almost everybody professes to value the idea of free speech. But many people will then insist on important exceptions that are almost always in vague language, which can have a broad range of meaning – the speech must not be disrespectful, offensive, hateful, harmful or damage reputations. These exceptions often effectively neuter free speech.

It can be argued that the High Court fell into this category. Despite invoking John Stuart Mill and making sound arguments about the centrality of academic freedom to a university, the High Court seemed to find it remarkably easy to take away that right, using the limitations of confidentiality and field of competence.

Nevertheless, the ruling has considerable value for the future, and despite the emotional and financial costs, and the technical loss, I am very happy to have had the opportunity to engage in the fight.

I cannot thank enough the IPA, and particularly John Roskam, Jennifer Marohasy, Gideon Rozner and Morgan Begg for their support. None of it would have been possible without the donations from 10,000 people, and the magnificent effort of the legal team. Most importantly, my wife Cheryl requires special thanks. She had to endure the horrible pressure and was always a source of good advice and rock-solid support.

1   *Ridd v James Cook University* [2021] HCA 32.

2   All the consultancy funds were used by the university to support student scholarships and research. None of the funds went to Ridd personally.

3   J Waterhouse, B Schaffelke, R Bartley, R Eberhard, J Brodie, M Star, P Thorburn, J Rolfe, M Ronan, B Taylor, and F Kroon, *2017 Scientific Consensus Statement: Land Use Impacts on Great Barrier Reef Water Quality and Ecosystem Condition* (2017) <https://www.reefplan.qld.gov.au/__data/assets/pdf_file/0029/45992/2017-scientific-consensus-statement-summary.pdf>.

4   P Larcombe, and P Ridd, 'The need for a formalised system of Quality Control for environmental policy-science' (2018) 126 *Marine Pollution Bulletin*, 449–461; P Larcombe, and P Ridd, 'Viewpoint: The need for a formalised system of Quality Assurance for Environmental Policy-Science and for improved policy advice to Government on the Great Barrier Reef. Reply to "Support for improved quality control but misplaced criticism of GBR science" by Britta Schaffelke, Katharina Fabricius, Frederieke Kroon, Jon Brodie, Glenn De'ath, Roger Shaw, Diane Tarte, Michael Warne, Peter Thorburn (Marine Pollution Bulletin 129: 357-363, 2018)' (2019) 143 *Marine Pollution Bulletin* 50–57.

5   'Unreliable research: Trouble at the lab', *The Economist*, 19 October 2013.

6   JPA Ioannidis, 'Why Most Published Research Findings Are False' (2005) 2(8) *PLoS Medicine*, 124.

7   P Larcombe and P Ridd, *The Sedimentary Geoscience of the Great Barrier Reef Shelf – Context for Management of Dredge Material* (Queensland Port Association, 2015).

8   P Larcombe and P Ridd, 'The need for a formalised system of Quality Control for environmental policy-science' (2018) 126 *Marine Pollution Bulletin*, 449–461.

9   G Lloyd, 'Fears uni may sack marine scientist over comments on reef health' *The Australian* (online 26 August 2017) <https://www. theaustralian.com.au/higher-education/fears-uni-may-sack-marine-scientist-over-comments-on-reef-health/news-story/5d70061c8df60 15abfcb07552de461df>.

10   G Lloyd, 'James Cook University slapdown of Great Barrier Reef science critic heads to court' *The Australian* (online 21 November 2017) <https://www.theaustralian.com.au/higher-education/james-cook-university-slapdown-of-reef-science-critic-heads-to-court/ news-story/2be5ccecca2cab24a93662663655b13c>.

11   Editorial, 'Rediscovering crucial freedoms' *The Australian* (online 24 July 2020) <https://www.theaustralian.com.au/commentary/ editorials/rediscovering-crucial-freedoms/news-story/8c6733628c17 5e90068925c189e9a9fa>.

12   *Ridd v James Cook University* [2021] HCA 32 [52].

13   TD Clark, GD Raby, DG Roche, *et al.* 'Ocean acidification does not impair the behaviour of coral reef fishes' (2020) 577 *Nature* 370–375 <https://doi.org/10.1038/s41586-019-1903-y>.

14   M Enserink, 'Sea of Doubts', *Science* (online 6 May 2021) <https:// www.science.org/content/article/does-ocean-acidification-alter-fish-behavior-fraud-allegations-create-sea-doubt>.

15   G Alcorn, 'Peter Ridd's sacking pushes the limit of academic freedom', *The Guardian* (online 5 June 2018) <https://www. theguardian.com/commentisfree/2018/jun/05/peter-ridds-sacking-pushes-the-limit-of-academic-freedom>.

16   Raising a complaint or concern (Web Page) <https://www.teqsa.gov. au/raising-complaint-or-concern>.

Academic freedom in a system beyond repair?

Morgan Begg

—

Academic freedom by definition exists in and is affected by the institution of academia, and how we understand the mission and purpose of universities will affect how academic freedom is protected. This is not a new debate either – the famous English theologian John Henry Newman courted controversy in the 1850s for delivering a series of lectures in which he challenged the mission of that era's university.

The lectures expressed Newman's utilitarian view of education, which valued a university for its economic value. Newman believed that rather than things like "work-ready graduates", "scientific discoveries" and "ideas for new businesses", universities should focus on enriching the soul and elevating the intellectual tone of society; cultivating the public mind; purifying the national taste; supplying true principles to popular enthusiasm and fixed aims to popular aspiration; giving enlargement and sobriety to the ideas of the age; facilitating the exercise of political power; and refining the intercourse of private life.[1]

Such debates would be a significant departure from the kind of debate we are holding about universities today. Rather than enriching the soul, most academics reject the notion of the soul altogether. Instead of work-ready graduates, universities produce woke-ready graduates, groomed for life in academia, the bureaucracy, or as mid-level human resource officers in big business.

And the only new ideas for businesses coming out of universities are innovations on diversity, inclusion and equity policies, which give radical ideologues control over corporate Australia.

The establishment of universities in Australia was made in the spirit of the higher values expressed by Newman. At the time of the founding of the University of Sydney, William Charles Wentworth assured the New South Wales Legislative Council that the purpose of the new institution was "to enlighten the mind, to refine the understanding, to elevate the souls of our fellow-men". When the University of Adelaide was established in 1879, the minister of education in South Australia even referred to Newman's ideal of an intellectual education to enable the mind "to look out into the world right forward, steadily and truly".[2]

But in recent years this intellectual mission of universities has fallen by the wayside. The suppression of scientific debate on campus is a threat to the very purpose of universities as it was expressed at their establishment in Australia. This was represented most vividly by the High Court's manifestly absurd decision in *Ridd v James Cook University*, in which it unanimously validated the university's vengeful and censorious response to physics professor Peter Ridd's criticism of mainstream scientific research into the climate and the GBR.

The High Court's decision is founded on a misinterpretation of the employment contract, severe failures of logic in its reasoning, and a disinterest in the underlying issues that collectively endorse campus culture and make the task of restoring academic freedom and scientific enquiry in this country much more difficult than most people imagine.

The legal analysis

Ridd was employed by James Cook University (JCU) from 1989, including an appointment as the head of physics between 2009 and 2016. At the time of Ridd's dispute with the university, the employment relationship was regulated primarily by the *James Cook University Enterprise Agreement 2013–2016* (the enterprise agreement).

The enterprise agreement protected among other things the right to intellectual freedom. Separate to the enterprise agreement, Ridd was obliged to comply with the university's code of conduct, which imposed standards of behaviour on staff.[3]

How these two instruments interacted was central to the legal dispute between Ridd and JCU (and this was confined solely to the legal dispute as JCU only ever engaged with the question of intellectual freedom once the case reached the stage of legal proceedings, and did not give any regard for Ridd's intellectual freedom at any point prior to the termination of his employment).

The dispute centred on three clauses of the enterprise agreement. The first was Clause 14, which defines the commitment of JCU to "act in manner consistent with the protection and promotion of intellectual freedom within the University and in accordance with JCU's code of conduct." This includes the right of staff to *inter alia* "pursue critical and open inquiry" and "participate in public debate and express opinions about issues and ideas related to their respective fields of competence".

Clause 14.3 of the enterprise agreement specifically explains:

> All staff have the right to express unpopular or controversial views. However, this comes with a responsibility to respect the rights of others and they do not have the right to harass, vilify, bully or intimidate those who disagree with their views. These rights are linked to the responsibilities of staff to support JCU as a place of independent learning and thought where ideas may be put forward and opinion expressed freely.

The phrases "in accordance with JCU's Code of Conduct", and "responsibility to respect the rights of others" were the basis of JCU's argument. JCU would argue that this implied that JCU was committed to making a code of conduct under which the right to intellectual opinion could be circumscribed by outlining how to respect the rights of others.

This was in conflict with Clause 13 of the enterprise agreement, which sets out the commitment of JCU to provide for a code of conduct. Specifically, it says, "The parties to this Agreement support the code of conduct as it establishes the standard by which staff and volunteers conduct themselves towards others and perform their professional duties on behalf of JCU" and to ensure that staff, among other things, "behave with respect to others". But importantly this commitment itself is limited. It provides under Clause 13.3 that "The parties note that the Code of Conduct is not intended to detract from Clause 14, Intellectual Freedom." In addition, section 29 of the *Fair Work Act* provides that, to the extent of any inconsistency, the "enterprise agreement prevails over a law of a State or a Territory", which includes the provisions of the *Public Sector Ethics Act 1994*, which enforces codes of conduct in public sector entities.

Given this, JCU actually had it completely backwards; rather than providing the means by which the code of conduct would circumscribe the right to intellectual freedom, a plain English reading of the enterprise agreement clauses appear to suggest that any code of conduct between JCU and staff is intended to be consistent with the university's commitment to protect intellectual freedom.

At its first hearing, the Federal Circuit Court agreed with this, upholding Ridd's claim that the university's disciplinary actions and findings had contravened the protection for intellectual freedom. Justice Salvatore Vasta made declarations of numerous contraventions of the enterprise agreement and ordered the university to pay Peter compensation totalling about $1.2 million.

On appeal to the Full Court of the Federal Court, a majority – comprised of Justices Griffiths and Derrington – agreed with JCU that none of the university's actions breached the enterprise agreement. The High Court differed slightly in its reasons but handed down the same result. The result was absurd for its incoherence in applying the rules only to Ridd, which could just as appropriately been applied to JCU. It made inappropriate findings in relation to private messages and emails; misinterpreted the provisions in the enterprise agreement relating to confidentiality; and failed to understand the underlying issue about academic freedom.

a)   The incoherence of only Ridd paying the price

The High Court rejected JCU's narrow interpretation of intellectual freedom. Instead, the court declared that intellectual freedom encompassed academic freedom which could not be restricted by "any asserted 'right' of others to [be given] respect or courtesy" and that the "purpose of intellectual freedom must permit of expression that departs from those civil norms."[4]

In applying these principles, the High Court did hold that JCU's decision to discipline and censure Ridd was unlawful in two respects:

1. the court held that JCU's 2016 censure of Ridd for a 2015 email he sent to a journalist in which he criticised scientific organisations such as the Great Barrier Reef Marine Park Authority (GBRMPA) and the ARC Centre for Excellence for Coral Reef Studies (CECRS) was held to be not justified and should not have occurred, and

2. the court held that JCU's 2017 censure of Ridd for failing to be respectful, courteous, and collegial by criticising major scientific organisations during an interview on Sky News in May 2017 was again held to be unjustified by the High Court according to its interpretation of the enterprise agreement.

So ultimately the High Court identified a couple of major breaches of the enterprise agreement by JCU, breaches that were foundational to the whole dispute.

And yet JCU did not pay a cost, only Ridd did.

It would perhaps be putting it lightly to say this is completely incoherent. It is also a failure to apply the law. Section 50 of the *Fair Work Act 2009* provides that "A person must not contravene a term of an enterprise agreement." Section 529 of the same act outlines that a serious contravention could be as high as 600 penalty units – or about $133,000 – or 60 penalty units for a non-serious breach, whatever that means.

In other words, the High Court identified breaches of the enterprise agreement, but didn't impose the penalty that is outlined in the legislation. This ought to be regarded as scandalous and brings into doubt how the High Court views the rule of law, to say the least.

To justify this inconsistency the High Court created a bizarre new criterion for Ridd that, because they felt he was making an all-or-nothing case, his failure to prove every part of his case meant none of the individual breaches carried legal consequences.

The judges even refer to how "the cases for both of the parties were conducted on an all-or-nothing basis". So both JCU and Ridd were supposedly running all-or-nothing arguments, which begs the question – what did it mean for JCU who failed to justify every disciplinary action, finding, or direction? The answer is it meant nothing. The High Court agreed that JCU acted unlawfully in some key respects, and Ridd paid the whole price for what the High Court believed was a failure to dispute each and every finding of serious misconduct.

b) Findings in relation to private messages and emails

As noted, Ridd failed to successfully dispute each and every finding of misconduct by the university, though these findings by the High Court were fundamentally erroneous.

The first set of findings made by JCU (findings 3 to 8) were based on the discovery of emails in which Ridd emailed what the High Court euphemistically describe as "external recipients" but was actually a couple of Ridd's former students. In those emails Ridd remarked that he had offended "powerful organisations" and "some sensitive but powerful and ruthless egos" and that "our whole university system pretends to value free debate, but in fact it crushes it".

The High Court argued – without much discussion at all – that these comments were not expressions of opinion within an area of Ridd's academic competence and therefore did not fall within the intellectual freedom protected by the enterprise agreement.

This finding by the High Court speaks to the shallowness of its inquiry. That these emails were only discovered after JCU went on a fishing expedition by brazenly scouring his email account for offending content, were not at all considered noteworthy by the court. No consideration was given to the fact that in enforcing the code of conduct, and to "protect the rights of others", JCU in effect ensured that the supposedly harmful content was entered into the public domain as part of high-profile legal proceedings. In reality, the only party that was responsible for spreading content that failed to respect the rights of others was JCU in digging up Ridd's private communications.

A semi-rigorous inquiry into JCU's conduct would have acknowledged even if this was permitted it was certainly unethical and disproportionate and ought to have weighed against the university in the High Court's final decision.

c) Confidentiality

The remainder of the findings are based on a repeated failure to "comply with his obligations with respect to confidentiality."[5] This finding implies that Ridd was subject to obligations of confidentiality and that his failure to abide by this obligation would justify findings of serious misconduct.

Not only is this wrong, it may be the most obscene of the High Court's findings. There was no basis under the code of conduct or the enterprise agreement for JCU issuing the kinds of confidentiality directions that it did. None.

At each stage of the disciplinary processes, from 2016 to 2018, JCU asserted that Ridd was subject to an obligation to maintain confidentiality of the disciplinary processes that he was being subjected to, as well as previous findings and censures handed down by the university.

Two subclauses of the enterprise agreement are relevant. The first is Clause 54.1.1, which provides that "the principles of procedural fairness and natural justice will be applied to all Misconduct and Serious Misconduct processes outlined in this clause." This will be important in a moment.

The second is Clause 54.1.5, which provides that the "confidentiality of all parties involved in the management of Misconduct and Serious Misconduct processes will be respected and all information gathered and recorded will remain confidential" subject to any obligations there may be to disclose information under legislation or other rules.

The argument that the confidentiality obligations should be interpreted to protect the university is, on the face of it, an extraordinary claim. First, the wording of the provision itself supports the alternative argument, that it is the university who bears the obligation to respect confidentiality. For instance, the reference to "all information gathered and recorded will remain confidential" only makes sense to apply to JCU because they are the only party gathering or recording information.

Second, Clause 54.1.5(C) provides that a person can give written consent to the university to release any information it collects or records. This suggests that, since the university is collecting or recording information, it has a responsibility to keep it confidential, but that a person can nonetheless disclose it themselves or let the university disclose any information.

This view is supported by the more fundamental principle

outlined in Clause 54.1.1 that the principles of procedural fairness and natural justice will be applied to all serious misconduct processes.

Natural justice and procedural fairness are principles designed for the benefit of parties who are subject to a disciplinary process or may be penalised by a process. For instance, in the context of criminal law, a court has a duty to act fairly and observe rules against bias, rules of evidence and the right to a fair hearing, because the court has the power to convict a person as a criminal. Since it controls the process it establishes safeguards to protect justice and fairness. This establishes confidence that a legal system is achieving just outcomes rather than enabling or exercising arbitrary power. The enterprise agreement specifies that these same values are imported into the university to apply to its own disciplinary processes.

There is a no indication anywhere in the enterprise agreement that the obligation to maintain confidentiality could apply to anyone other than the university, because the university is the party that controls the process. It is in response to the danger of the university abusing its power that the principles for natural justice and procedural fairness are required.

In effect, what the High Court endorsed was JCU's argument that it can impose obligations of confidentiality on a person it was subjecting to its disciplinary process. In other words, the High Court was saying the application of natural justice principles meant the university could conduct secret trials.

A breach of sound legal principles and values of justice by the High Court is a scandal. And the High Court can't say simply that they didn't consider it because the very question was addressed by at least one judge when the case was heard in the Federal Court. Justice Rangiah highlighted that defining the confidentiality provisions in the enterprise agreement in the way JCU preferred:

Would reveal a Kafkaesque scenario of a person secretly accused and secretly found guilty of a disciplinary offence but unable to reveal, under threat of further secret charges being brought, that he or she had ever been charged and found guilty.[6]

This is exactly what occurred. Had Ridd complied with the farcical directions he would not have been able to obtain legal advice, he would not have been able to contact other organisations such as the Institute of Public Affairs for advice and support, and he would not have been allowed to appeal to the public for crowd-funded financial support, as any communication would have been a breach of confidentiality and generated further findings of serious misconduct.

d) The High Court missed the bigger point

The High Court's overall failure was a failure to understand the context of Ridd's case. It is difficult to conceive of how the case would have progressed to the point that it did if not for the subject matter of Ridd's expressions. In reality, the only reason Ridd was being targeted and ultimately terminated by the university was not because of some breach of confidentiality, or private emails to friends, but because of his stated and public views about the lack of intellectual rigour in scientific research into the GBR and the science of climate change.

It is not clear why a decision, based in part on actions of the university that were determined to be unlawful, was still considered to be legitimate by the High Court. JCU's decision to terminate Ridd's employment was, the High Court said, a culmination of a series of events. Tellingly, the very first in the series of events was the findings of serious misconduct and the first censure in 2016, which the High Court said was not lawful under the enterprise agreement. The censure in 2017 was a major event in a series of events and was also determined to be unlawful by the High Court. If one removes from the factual setting Ridd's protected commentary within his area of expertise, being commentary about scientific research and the GBR, it is reasonable to argue that the case would not have transpired this way at all. Had Ridd not been initially targeted for his genuine views in his area of expertise, he would never have seen the need to speak to others about what was happening to him, thereby breaching the confidentiality orders.

In short, the university's decision to dismiss Ridd was affected, and infected, by its own unlawful conduct.

The court's failures to consider each of the above factors could be regarded as disinterest. A cynic could be forgiven for assuming that the judges of the High Court were ultimately not engaged with the serious questions of censorship underlying a dispute in an employment contract because it has more esoteric ambitions. Namely in following the judicial tradition started by former High Courts of making its mark on the country through symbolic judgements about implied rights or by issuing landmark declarations about the nature of the settlement of Australia.[7]

This would explain for instance why it is that the judges committed a mere 65 paragraphs to blithely dismiss Ridd's appeal to an explicitly protected right to intellectual freedom in an employment contract. It would also explain how a little over a year earlier some of the same judges could collectively commit 468 paragraphs of abstruse legal reasoning to discover in the Australian Constitution a new category of citizenship based on the racial background of a person, as it did in the *Love/Thoms* case handed down in 2020.[8]

What this all means is that any marginal change to the governing legislation promising to protect academic or intellectual freedoms shouldn't be seen as a panacea to the problem of academic freedom[9] – not least because it would rely on the same academic administrators to enforce and the same courts to interpret a clear protection for intellectual freedom, which they have already demonstrated a failure to do.

Academia: a system beyond repair?

It should be said that a prerequisite to securing intellectual freedom for academics is that those in the academy must want the freedom in the first place. The difficulty is that many academics tend to be intellectually shallow and favour the existence and enforcement of conformist groupthink because it doesn't demand they ever defend or prove their beliefs, whatever they happen to be on the day. Academics today are satisfied to go along and be in the in-crowd, and will update their beliefs as required.

Case in point, two academics who wrote the book on academic freedom were Carolyn Evans and Adrienne Stone, who bemoaned the influence the IPA was having on public debate and for bringing awareness to the problem of free speech on campus. In their 2021 book *Open Minds: Academic Freedom and Freedom of Speech in Australia*, the writers assert that censorship in academia is largely historical and predominantly affects left-of-centre academics, and that more scope should be given to restricting academic freedom.

For instance, they suggest the definition of academic freedom should be limited to things which, they argue, are for academic purposes or for the functioning of a university. This would mean censoring speech that could "cause serious emotional harm", was "obviously untrue or even dangerous ideas", and which "denigrate[s] a group within the university". These would each be massive tools for university bureaucrats to wield against heterodox academics – academics like Peter Ridd.

In other words, the modern academic typically fails to live up to the ideal expressed by John Henry Newman, that a person with a university education should be prepared to:

> Fill any post with credit, and to master any subject with facility. It shows him how to accommodate himself to others, how to throw himself into their state of mind, how to bring before them his own, how to influence them, how to come to an understanding with them, how to bear with them.[10]

Our universities are not prepared to "bear with" differing views. This problem with our academics, and the failure to protect academic free speech, should be understood in the context of a broader systemic failure of the modern university model.

The Australian university sector is as monolithic as it is ossified. The stifling of academic freedom is so widespread in Australia because the modern university system is an assortment of oligopolist entities who are effectively identical in what they teach and how they operate. Much of this is due to the institutions being subject to the stringent rules of the national regulator, the Tertiary Education Quality and Standards Agency (TEQSA). But this has been a problem even prior to the establishment of TEQSA – in 1988 Claudio Veliz identified the fundamental lack of diversity in the sector:

> Australia [has] one of the least diversified higher education systems of any major Western democracy; her 20 universities are administered largely in the same

manner, using comparable salary scales, similar career structures, and with most other internal administrative and academic arrangements, standardised or modified in consultation with the central authorities. It is only a gentle exaggeration to say that Australia has one huge university with 20 campuses strewn over her vast territory.[11]

The other systemic problem is that the modern universities are first and foremost corporatised entities. The pursuit of truth is subsidiary to not only maintaining lucrative government or corporate partnerships (such as those maintained by JCU with the CECRS or the GBRMPA) but to maximising revenue by ensuring the widest number of applicants are able to enter and graduate from their system. That their fees are guaranteed by the federal government or paid in full by foreign students just means universities carry negligible risk by admitting as many students as possible.

This is both reinforced by and reinforces the over-credentialisation of society. The informal national policy that the maximum number of young people *must* go to university in order to fully participate in the economy and society inevitably runs into the reality that not all young people are suited to tertiary studies.

As a result of these factors, we now have too many universities that have a limitless pool of potential students. So much so that they do not need to compete with each other to attract students so are not motivated to be a place of superior intellectualism. Inevitably, standards are reduced across the board to accommodate the influx of applicants and over time this leads to the dumbing down of academic standards.

Rather than correcting this, the way research is funded reinforces the diminished state of intellectual inquiry. As exposed in an important chapter of the IPA's 2020 book *Climate Change:*

The Facts, Dr Paul McFayden, Dr Bella d'Abrera and Scott Hargreaves explain how the present model of government research grants form what they call an "Iron Triangle", a self-reinforcing phenomenon in which research that promotes alarmist findings on climate change are incentivised.

Because research funding is distributed as blocks of time-limited grants, the researchers are incentivised to devote a significant amount of their time to promoting the cause for which they are given funding. As they explain, one of the problems in this dynamic is that the purchaser of research is an elected government:

> There were a few problems the policy bureaucrats had overlooked. The purchaser – provider economic model requires an *informed* purchaser for the model to work effectively. In this transaction, however, the most informed person is the scientist and researcher – the provider – rather than the purchaser, or government. This gives the provider the capacity to manipulate the purchaser and can lead to adverse outcomes ...

> The second problem is that the purchaser in democratic countries is an elected government. Scientists know that the way to get government to fund their research is by harnessing scare campaigns using the green pressure groups and the media ...

> So instead of government having control over the direction of scientific research, the application of competitive market economics by grant funding has influenced the establishment of a science funding model of interacting and reinforcing self-interest groups.

This has reduced government flexibility and made government policy hostage to the scientific organisations and pressure groups. This model is now largely the way science, including climate science, is funded in government scientific institutions and universities.[12]

Ridd himself said in an email to a former student that he was in strife with the university because he offended some "powerful organisations". He was evidently right. The kinds of views that Ridd expressed are a threat to the very business model of the research–university complex that has been constructed around government funding. Not only was he driven out of his job for it, the High Court approved their actions, endorsing the worst instincts and practices of academic cancel culture in the process.

1   JH Newman, *The Idea of University: Defined and Illustrated* (Longmans, Green, and Co., 1907) 177-8.

2   S Chavura, 'Culture, Utility, and Critique: The Idea of University in Australia,' in W Colman (ed.) *Campus Meltdown: The Deepening Crisis in Australian Universities* (Connor Court Publishing, 2019) 214.

3   The *Public Sector Ethics Act 1994* (QLD) provides for codes of conduct to express standards of conduct for public sector entities. The schedule to the *Public Sector Ethics Act* provides under the definition of a "public sector entity" a "university established under an Act or an agricultural college". James Cook University is established under the *James Cook University Act 1997* (QLD).

4   *James Cook University v Ridd* [2021] HCA 32 [33].

5   Ibid [53].

6   *James Cook University v Ridd* [2020] FCAFC 123, 72 [276].

7   *Nationwide News Pty Ltd v Wills* (1992) 177 CLR 1 (implied right to political communication); *Mabo v Queensland (No 2)* (1992) 175 CLR 1.

8   *Love v Commonwealth; Thoms v Commonwealth* [HCA] 3; M Begg, 'Courting Calamity' (2020) 72(2) *IPA Review* 35-42.

9   See for instance the *Higher Education Support Amendment (Freedom of Speech) Act 2021*, which incorporated into the *Higher Education Support Act 2003* an expanded definition of academic freedom and requires every Australian university to have a policy protecting freedom of speech that aligns with the model code contained in the Report of the Independent Review of Freedom of Speech in Australian Higher Education Providers (2019) ("The French Code").

10   Newman, 178.

11   See S Hargreaves, "Two Cheers for Uni Reform" (2021) 73(4) *IPA Review* 57-61.

12   P McFayden, S Hargreaves, and B d'Abrera, 'Of Blind Beetles and Shapeshifting Birds: Research Grants and Climate Catastrophism' in J Marohasy (ed), *Climate Change: The Facts 2020* (Institute of Public Affairs, 2020) 294-5.

A pyrrhic victory for James Cook University

Chris Merritt

—

In October last year when the High Court handed down a short, unanimous decision in Peter Ridd's case, the true victor in this fight over academic freedom was hard to identify. Neither of the official parties would have been entirely happy with the outcome. After 27 years at James Cook University (JCU), Ridd had failed to overturn his dismissal; and the university had been left with a big legal bill and a judgement that identified its improper attempts to silence a world-class professor of physics.

Officially, JCU won this case. But it's a pyrrhic victory.

The High Court broke with normal practice and refused to order Ridd to pay the university's costs. That in itself was quite a blow; the university had been represented by Bret Walker SC, who does not come cheap. But it lost something far more important than money – the reputation of this institution has been trashed.

The world has been left with the impression that this university does not understand the principle that lies at the heart of the scientific method: when searching for the truth, robust debate must prevail over courtesy. That taint will be difficult to remove.

So to describe this organisation as a winner does not capture the full impact of what happened.

When viewed from Ridd's perspective the outcome of this dispute is utterly unjust. On the substantive issue of academic freedom, he was shown to be right, and the university was shown to be wrong.

It was wrong to try to temper his criticism of what he considered to be shoddy science. Yet the wrongdoers still managed to salvage a victory. And one of the factors that contributed to that outcome is right out of Kafka: Ridd had failed to respect the confidentiality of an improper disciplinary process that targeted his legitimate right to engage in robust professional discourse.

On one level, the wrongdoers won after changing the terms of the dispute. They shifted it from a principled argument about academic freedom to a bureaucratic argument about the requirements of the university's disciplinary process. Once that process was under way, the court decided that Ridd was obliged to remain silent about that process. He did not. And who could blame him? From his perspective it would have been a continuation of the university's campaign to silence someone who had challenged the orthodoxy on global warming and the health of the GBR.

But there was another factor at play – one that leaves the impression that the High Court's judgement was infected by a misconception about the nature of the argument that had been presented to the court. If that is the case, there is also a prospect that this case was wrongly decided.

But before examining that point, it needs to be made clear that this judgement falls into two halves. For Ridd, who fought to defend his right to speak robustly on matters within his field of expertise, the court's failure to overturn his dismissal is an injustice that many will find inexplicable.

It sits uncomfortably with the other half of this judgement that consists of an entirely persuasive exposition on the importance of academic freedom and why robust debate must prevail over bureaucratic demands for courtesy and collegiality.

This part of the judgement is a foundation for action by whoever happens to be education minister in the next federal government.[1] If the next minister takes up the challenge, the real winners will be future generations – not just academics but all those who benefit from academic rigour.

This part of the decision is also a warning to university bureaucrats who might be tempted to muzzle other academics. The nation's highest court is united on the importance of intellectual freedom and, barring more judicial misconceptions, it seems inclined to side with academics should this issue again come before the court.

That, of course, assumes that other academics would have the fortitude and resources to follow Ridd's example and fight for the right to speak their mind. That is quite an assumption. In the real world, it would be a rare soul who would be prepared to risk their employment and finances in a fight over an issue of principle.

There is always a public and a private interest in protecting freedom of speech. But with academic freedom, which is a category of freedom of speech, the public interest in protecting this right predominates. It outweighs any assertion that people need to be protected from the risk of professional embarrassment when shoddy work is exposed. The public interest in exposing bad science must prevail.

That is why the next federal government needs to ensure academics will never again need to resort to private litigation to defend their right to engage in robust professional discourse. Government has a duty to protect the public interest in academic rigour.

We have already seen how government action can nudge universities in the right direction through the development of a voluntary code on academic freedom by former High Court Chief Justice Robert French.

But while a voluntary code might help, it is not a silver bullet. These codes fail to take account of the fact that universities are in the business of education. And like all businesses, they are sensitive to threats to their revenue and anything that could annoy influential stakeholders. So, while voluntary codes are welcome, they are unlikely to prove decisive when public discourse by academics and students is viewed as a threat to the interests of tertiary institutions.

In his 2019 review of academic freedom, French was wary of damaging institutional autonomy. He believed a statutory standard on academic freedom, beyond the level of generality currently reflected in the higher education standards made under the *Tertiary Education Quality Standards Agency Act 2011*, would be disproportionate to any threat to freedom of expression that exists or is likely to exist on Australian university campuses for the foreseeable future.[2] As is well-known, French favoured the voluntary approach.

But is that good enough? How realistic is it to expect a voluntary code to make a difference when academic freedom threatens relations with key stakeholders or financial backers?

This is much more than a theoretical issue. Remember Drew Pavlou? In 2020, when he was an arts student at The University of Queensland, he was suspended for two years – which was subsequently reduced to six months – for protesting against Chinese government influence on Australian university campuses.

The influence of the Chinese Communist Party within the university was a feature of the report on this incident that appeared in the *Los Angeles Times*. After Pavlou was jostled for his anti-China views, the US newspaper reported that on the day after the protest Chinese state media named Pavlou as a leader of the protest. The *LA Times* report said:

> Xu Jie, Beijing's consul general in Brisbane, praised the "spontaneous patriotic behavior" of those who had attacked him.[3]

It was an unusual statement for a diplomat, especially considering Xu's other position – adjunct professor at the university's School of Languages and Cultures. His dual roles were an example of the increasingly close ties between Australian universities and China, their biggest source of international students.

The university didn't chastise Xu for promoting violence. Instead, it defended its relationship with Beijing – and turned on one of its brightest students.

The Chinese Communist Party had no role in Ridd's case, but Ridd suspected other outside entities. The judgement shows he sent emails outlining his suspicion that he had offended "powerful organisations" and "some sensitive but powerful and ruthless egos".

Five months before the High Court's ruling, the weakness of the French code was outlined by George Williams, the Deputy Vice-Chancellor of the University of NSW. Williams pointed out that:

> The code permits universities to ban people from speaking on campus where their speech is likely to "involve the advancement of theories or propositions which purport to be based on scholarship or research but which fall below scholarly standards to such an extent as to be detrimental to the university's character as an institution of higher learning". Universities can use this clause to limit speech that would be lawful

off-campus, perhaps on topics such as climate change or vaccination. As a result, UNSW adopted the model code without this clause.[4]

This is why the next federal government cannot allow this issue to rest.[5] Unless the government takes up this issue, its inaction could be an invitation for another round of litigation.

Those who read the judgement in Ridd's case will find that JCU was wrong to censure Ridd over a 2015 email to a journalist that said the Great Barrier Reef Marine Park Authority was grossly misusing some scientific data to make the case that the reef was greatly damaged. The same email had criticised the ARC Centre of Excellence for Coral Reef Studies (CECRS), which then complained to JCU.

The court made the point that there was no suggestion that the remarks in the email were anything other than honestly held opinions. Nothing said in that email had ever been suggested to be unlawful, defamatory, wrong or even unreasonable.

Those who read the judgement will see that the university was also wrong to have censured Ridd in 2017 for remarks on Sky News in which he said it was no longer possible to trust research on the GBR from the Australian Institute of Marine Science and the CECRS.

The university was also found to be wrong to cite his remarks to Alan Jones and Peta Credlin on Sky News and tell him his intellectual freedom did not extend to criticising "key stakeholders of the university" in a manner that was not "respectful and courteous".

Ridd's remarks during that interview led to a declaration by the university that he was guilty of serious misconduct. Yet legal academics later came to the view that it was no more than a conventional exercise of academic freedom.[6] So what was it that so annoyed the university's decision makers? In essence an academic had merely engaged in the time-honoured practice of criticising the research of other academics.

While being interviewed, Ridd affirmed remarks he had made in a book chapter, which argued that the GBR "[q]uietly grows and waits for the beginning of the next cycle of death and regrowth".

He added that after the reef "crashes", the "scientists ... then do the same stories and push it all around the world again". He said that "this has been going on for close to 50 years, how many more years will it take for us to cotton-on to the fact that you can no longer trust this stuff, unfortunately".

Earlier in that interview he had said:

> ... the basic problem is that we can no longer trust the scientific organisations like the Australian Institute of Marine Science, even things like the ARC Centre of Excellence for Coral Reef Studies. A lot of this stuff is coming out, the science is coming not properly checked, tested or replicated and this is a great shame because we really need to be able to trust our scientific institutions. And the fact is, I do not think we can anymore.

> I think that most of the scientists who are pushing out this stuff, they genuinely believe that there are problems with the reef. I just don't think that they are very objective about the science they do. I think [they're] emotionally attached to their subject, and ... You know you can't blame them, the reef is a beautiful thing.[7]

At its core, Ridd's fight was over his right to engage in this kind of robust discourse regardless of whether he hurt the feelings of those whose work he was criticising. This goes beyond the issue of whether the reef is or is not in trouble – however important that might be. It goes to the issue of whether it is possible for the fate of the GBR to be freely discussed by experts without fear of retribution.

Underlying the entire dispute were two documents that took different approaches to academic freedom. The university's enterprise agreement granted staff the right to express unpopular and controversial views and pursue critical and open inquiry. But a separate code of conduct required intellectual freedom to be exercised with courtesy and respect – terms not found in the enterprise agreement.

After considering Ridd's statements to Jones and Credlin, the court determined they provided no basis for disciplinary action. This was a clear rejection of the university's argument that his intellectual freedom did not justify what it said was "criticism of key stakeholders of the university" in a manner that was not "in the collegial and academic spirit of the search for knowledge, understanding and truth" or "respectful and courteous".

Ridd lost the case for several reasons: the first is that the enterprise agreement only protected his right to make statements within his area of professional expertise and he had sent emails to external recipients that did not come within that definition. Those emails asserted that he had offended "powerful organisations" and "some sensitive but powerful and ruthless egos", and that "our whole university system pretends to value free debate, but in fact it crushes it".

From Ridd's perspective, the requirement to remain silent about the disciplinary process would have been seen as an illegitimate continuation of the university's attack on his right to express his professional opinion. He also appeared to be protected by provisions in the university's enterprise agreement that give academics the right to "express opinions about the operations of

JCU" and "to express disagreement with university decisions and with the processes used to make those decisions".

It is therefore not surprising that he refused to play along. Had he done so, it would have meant accepting that bureaucrats had the right to muzzle an academic who, according to the High Court's judgement, has been ranked within the top 5 per cent of researchers globally.

After the judgement was handed down Ridd described the secrecy provision of the complaint-handling mechanism as "Stasi-like". This is what he told Andrew Bolt on Sky News:

> In the end I was sick and tired of being told what I was or was not allowed to say. I knew I was taking a risk on that confidentiality but it just had to be done.

> There was just no choice; I couldn't live with myself and just shut up, which is what I would have had to have done.[8]

The bizarre nature of this secrecy trap was not lost on those who were following this affair. Soon after the High Court's ruling, academics from Melbourne University wrote that one way of summarising the court's decision was that Ridd's termination was justified by his repeated failure to respect the confidentiality of a disciplinary process that should never have been commenced.

The IPA's Morgan Begg, writing in *The Australian*, came to the same conclusion. He wrote that the implication from the ruling was that the university could launch an unlawful investigation of an employee, but it would be entirely lawful to force the employee to keep that investigation secret.[9]

Logically, it seems hard to reconcile the court's view that confidentiality should prevail over disciplinary procedures with its view, in the same judgement, that courtesy and collegiality should not prevail over robust professional discourse. Using this logic, Ridd had the right to express his professional opinion discourteously but not to disclose his view that his right to do so had been violated.

The secrecy trap is by no means the most troubling aspect of this decision. That honour is reserved for the reference in paragraph six of the judgement that says:

> ... as senior counsel for Dr Ridd frankly accepted in his oral reply, the cases for both of the parties were conducted on *an all-or-nothing basis*. From Dr Ridd's perspective, this forensic choice reflected the reality that, unless he was able to show that all, or almost all of the actions by JCU were contraventions of cl 14 [of the enterprise agreement] then the termination of his employment would have been justified and would have occurred in any event leaving him with little benefit had he sought to uphold only a few of the instances of declared contraventions.[10] [Emphasis added]

Here's the problem: It was never part of Ridd's pleaded case that unless he succeeded in every respect, he did not wish to prevail in any respect. The transcript of oral argument before the court shows there are just two occasions where the words "all or nothing" appear. And a reasonable reading of that part of the transcript leaves the clear impression that the reference was a statement about the logic of the parties' construction of Clause 14 of the enterprise agreement and its application to the university's direction that the disciplinary proceedings should remain confidential. It cannot be read as a concession that none of Ridd's claims should succeed unless all of them were successful. Yet that is how Ridd's argument is portrayed in paragraph six of the judgement.

Here is the relevant section of the transcript, which starts with counsel for Ridd, Stuart Wood KC:

> MR WOOD: Some short points, if it pleases the court … It was never argued that the breach of confidentiality directions by themselves – in answer to Justice Edelman's question – would constitute serious misconduct. There was no finding below that they would constitute serious misconduct and the reason for that was it was *all or nothing* for the university. They said we have the test right, you have it wrong, the code of conduct is the thing that governs everything, and Clause 14 [of the enterprise agreement] has nothing to do with it.
>
> JUSTICE EDELMAN: It was *all or nothing* for your client as well.
>
> MR WOOD: Of course, of course – both ways. But if we are correct in terms of our construction of Clause 14 then the directions [for confidentiality] go too far because they contravene the Clause 14 rights and they also attempt to suppress – and are thereby unlawful – communication, publication of an unlawful process.[11] [Emphasis added]

If my reading of the transcript is correct, it suggests that the "all-or-nothing" reference has been misunderstood by the court as being a concession by Ridd's counsel that, in fact, was never made. The transcript does not show that Ridd was prepared to concede every aspect of the case unless he won every separate point. Such a move would defy logic as it would not serve Ridd's interests.

It is difficult to avoid the conclusion that the exchange between Stuart Wood KC and Justice Edelman, quoted above, concerned the proper construction of clause 14 of the enterprise agreement and its application to the confidentiality directions that had been made by the university.

So if a broad "all-or-nothing" concession was never made, the court's formal decision to give the university an unqualified victory must be in doubt. This is due to the fact that the judgement makes it clear that Ridd was right on the core issue of his freedom to express his professional opinion even when he did so in a robust and discourteous manner. Keep in mind that Ridd had sought a range of remedies, including declarations, penalties and compensation.

Once the limited nature of the "all-or-nothing" reference is properly understood, the logical consequence is that Ridd should have been entitled to at least some remedies – including formal declarations – for those actions that were taken against him by the university that the court clearly believed were unlawful. This would be the case even if his dismissal were still found to be lawful.

Before leaving the "all-or-nothing" point, I want to make it clear that my attention was drawn to this issue by a senior lawyer who was passing on information from an even more senior lawyer. They both wanted this issue to be made public but were not prepared to put their names to this critique of a unanimous ruling by the High Court. However, the hearing transcript tells the story.

The fact that Ridd needed to litigate in order to defend academic freedom was the result of a form of groupthink that is creeping through universities not just in this country but through the traditional centres of Western Civilisation. Douglas Murray, in his book *The War on the West*, says a new generation does not appear to understand even the most basic principles of free thought and free expression and how the scientific method has improved the lives of countless people around the world. Murray puts it down to a cultural war within the centres of Western Civilisation in which almost everything of importance that has emerged from the West is viewed with suspicion.

According to Murray:

> ... everything connected with the Western tradition is being jettisoned. At education colleges in America, aspiring teachers have been given training seminars where they are taught that even the term "diversity of opinion" is "white supremacist bullshit".

So what is to be done?

Ridd might have lost his personal fight, but it was just one battle in a much broader war in which freedom of speech and other core Western values are at stake. But Ridd was not fighting alone. Some of the greatest thinkers from the Western cultural tradition feature in the High Court's judgement, including philosopher and jurist Ronald Dworkin from the United States.

On the day of the ruling, education minister Alan Tudge made the point that 41 universities had aligned their policies on free speech with French's model code. In the view of the former Chief Justice, academic freedom is a defining characteristic of universities – an assessment that was cited by the High Court along with the classical defence of free speech by John Stuart Mill.

According to Mill's great essay, On Liberty, while a prohibition upon disrespectful and discourteous conduct in intellectual expression might be a "convenient plan for having peace in the intellectual world", the "price paid for this sort of intellectual pacification, is the sacrifice of the entire moral courage of the human mind".[12]

When we look a little deeper at French's report on academic freedom, the former Chief Justice makes it explicit that the idea of academic freedom has roots that go all the way back to the heart of Western Civilisation, ancient Greece.

According to the French report:

> The ideal of academic freedom can be traced back to Socrates' defence in Plato's Apology, before the Athenian people, of his right to discuss controversial topics with others, that those in power found unacceptable.[13]

Despite George Williams' concerns about the shortcomings of French's model code, there is no doubt it is a step in the right direction; however, there clearly need to be more steps. More than two years before the judgement, Ridd praised the code and called for it to be made mandatory at all universities, not voluntary.[14]

On the day of the judgement the education minister recognised that in some places there is a culture of closing down perceived "unwelcome thoughts" rather than debating them.[15] This is in line with Williams' concern that governments and public institutions have become less tolerant of freedom of speech and more willing to deny people their voice. He attributes a good part of the problems to the nation's parliaments, which have enacted an ever-growing list of anti-speech laws.

On free speech, Williams is the polar opposite of the bureaucrats at JCU who tried to silence Ridd. Williams believes freedom of speech on campus should be no different to freedom of speech everywhere in Australia. The only constraints should be those that apply under the normal law such as defamation. But while Ridd favours a mandatory code on free speech at universities, Williams goes much further. He believes the entire community needs stronger protection for freedom of speech. According to Williams:

We need a free speech statute that applies across our society to provide every person with a right of free expression. This should apply a common standard to universities and other parts of our society to ensure consistent and effective protection for a vital democratic value.[16]

The conduct of JCU is not an isolated incident. It is part of a cultural war that is being fought in those countries that have been built on core ideas from the Western tradition. Free speech is one of those ideas, but so is religious liberty and, most importantly, the rule of law. But all of those freedoms depend on the first – freedom of speech.

Ridd lost his personal battle. But he secured a unanimous ruling from the High Court that provides a foundation for the future defence of academic freedom. The court recognised that this doctrine has an instrumental as well as an ethical justification. It aids the search for truth in the contested marketplace for ideas. It also ensures the primacy of individual conviction – the right not to profess what one believes to be false while bestowing a duty to speak out for what one believes.[17]

The starting point for future battles will be the voluntary codes. But ranged against them is the reality that universities have powerful stakeholders who can influence these organisations in a variety of ways.

One former vice-chancellor told me that those in charge of the nation's universities are, in the main, terrified that their staff will do or say something that could jeopardise commercial relationships or imperil future grants. In this person's assessment, that is merely part of a broader problem in which academics who challenge the dominant paradigm risk being sidelined. Groupthink, in this person's view, is just as big an enemy of academic freedom as the institutional self-interest of universities.

Robert French was clearly right to be wary about eroding the autonomy of the universities. But that horse has already bolted. The autonomy of these organisations has already been abridged by influential outside stakeholders – just as Ridd feared. Also at play are the contending forces of the cultural war that is under way within the nations of the West. The challenge confronting the federal government is to decide how to ensure these influences do not undermine academic freedom. Is it good enough to limit academic freedom to discussion within a person's area of expertise? Such an approach still accepts that universities can legitimately stifle public discussion and will encourage timidity.

The next federal government might do well to re-examine George Williams' proposal for broader statutory protection for free speech regardless of whether it takes place on campus, in academic journals, or on television. The government might also care to revisit the definition of academic freedom that French had proposed in his report. It included several uncontroversial elements as well as components that would protect statements made within an academic's field of expertise. French had also included one provision that would have endorsed the right of academics to speak freely in their personal capacity on any issue without constraint by their employer. This provision says academic freedom includes:

> The freedom of academic staff, without constraint imposed by reason of their employment by the

university, to make lawful public comment on any issue in their personal capacities ...[18]

This would have eliminated the risk that future disputes would turn on the question of whether statements are permissible because they are within an academic's area of expertise or impermissible because they fall outside a notional boundary. By protecting "lawful public comment on any issue" the French proposal would have eliminated that boundary. It would therefore also have eliminated the risk of litigation over the extent of the boundary. It would have prevented university bureaucrats from attempting to regulate public statements that academics might make in their personal capacities.

So what happened to that proposal? In March 2021, federal parliament approved amendments to the *Higher Education Support Act 2003* to implement recommendations from the French report, including the report's definition of academic freedom. Every element of French's proposed definition was included in the amendment – except the provision outlined above that would have protected lawful public comment on any issue. The amendment was made in the Higher Education Support Amendment (Freedom of Speech) Bill 2020. The explanatory memorandum to the bill says:

The statutory definition in Item 4 closely aligns with the definition in the French Model Code but includes a minor technical modification recommended by the University Chancellors Council, in consultation with the Honourable Robert French AC. This modification excludes from the definition "the freedom of academic staff, without constraint imposed by reason of their employment by the university, to make lawful public comment on any issue in their personal capacities" element of the Code definition. This element of the definition was more appropriately considered to fit within the ambit of a broader societal freedom, referred to in the Model Code as "freedom of speech", rather than within the narrower concept of "academic freedom".[19]

The decision to eliminate part of the proposed definition of academic freedom might have served the interests of the University Chancellors' Council but it has reduced the potential benefits for academics. When a future education minister addresses this issue, the thoughts of Ronald Dworkin, as embraced by the High Court in the Ridd judgement, could be a sound guiding principle:

> The idea that people have that right [to protection from speech that might reasonably be thought to embarrass or lower others' esteem for them or their own self-respect] is absurd. Of course it would be good if everyone liked and respected everyone else who merited that response. But we cannot recognize a right to respect, or a right to be free from the effects of speech that makes respect less likely, without wholly subverting the central ideals of the culture of independence and denying the ethical individualism that that culture protects.[20]

---

1 The Syposium took place prior to the 2022 federal election.

2 Department of Education and Training (Cth), *Report of the Independent Review of Freedom of Speech in Australian Higher Education Providers* (2019) 222.

3 S Bengali and M Petrakis, 'An Australian student denounced his university's ties to China. Then he became a target', *Los Angeles Times*, 21 December 2020.

4 G Williams, 'Free speech code for unis should apply nationwide', *The Australian*, 7 June 2021.

5   The Symposium into *The Future of Scientific Enquiry and Academic Freedom* was held on 13 May 2022, just prior to the May 2022 federal election in which the Coalition government was defeated.

6   J Forrest and A Stone, 'The High Court's defence of academic freedom in Ridd v JCU', *Australian Public Law*, 17 November 2021.

7   *Ridd v James Cook University* [2021] HCA 32, [48].

8   Sky News, 'Commonwealth 'intervention' is the 'only way' to protect academic free speech', *The Bolt Report*, 13 October 2021 (Peter Ridd).

9   M Begg, 'Ruling against Ridd shines a light on cancel culture', *The Australian*, 13 October 2021.

10   *Ridd v James Cook University* [2021] HCA 32 at [6].

11   Transcript of Proceedings, *Ridd v James Cook University* [2021] HCATrans 110 (23 June 2021) 2355-2365.

12   JS Mill, *On Liberty*.

13   Department of Education and Training (Cth), *Report of the Independent Review of Freedom of Speech in Australian Higher Education Providers* (2019) 114.

14   P Ridd, 'Robert French's code is a beacon for freedom of speech', *The Australian*, 26 April 2019.

15   A Tudge, 'Statement: Ridd High Court decision' (Media release, 13 October 2021) <https://ministers.dese.gov.au/tudge/statement-ridd-high-court-decision>.

16   G Williams, 'Free speech code for unis should apply nationwide', *The Australian*, 7 June 2021.

17   *Ridd v James Cook University* [2021] HCA 32, [31], citing R Dworkin, 'We need a new interpretation of academic freedom' (1996) 82(3) Academe 10, 11.

18   Department of Education and Training (Cth), *Report of the Independent Review of Freedom of Speech in Australian Higher Education Providers* (2019) 231.

9   Explanatory Memorandum, Higher Education Support Amendment (Freedom of Speech) Bill 2020, 10.

20   Department of Education and Training (Cth), *Report of the Independent Review of Freedom of Speech in Australian Higher Education Providers* (2019) 222.

Universities and
turbulent academics

James Allan

—

I would like to begin by thanking the IPA and John Roskam for having invited me to write this chapter. John and the IPA have been true warriors in the cause of freedom for all my time here in Australia. I arrived in Australia in early 2005 and there was soon Andrew Bolt's supposed hate-speech case saga. Roskam and the IPA were there on the side of freedom. Likewise the QUT students' affair, when again we saw the IPA on the side of free speech and freedom; likewise Bill Leak's persecution – let's call it what it was – by the Human Rights Commission; likewise the last two years of the pandemic despotism with its (and I quote the retired UK Supreme Court Justice Lord Sumption) "greatest inroads on our civil liberties and freedoms in the last three hundred years" – and do not get me started on the fear porn press; the heavy-handed policing; the way billions of dollars were shifted from the young and the poor to the old and the rich (and the two pandemic years were the best years ever for billionaires); and how untold debts were racked up, which our grandkids will be paying off and how this led to asset inflation that helped, yes, those with assets; or how deaths caused by the lockdowns themselves – think missed cancer checks, mental health problems, the long-term effects of two missed years of schooling for those without smart middle-class mums at home to do the teachers' jobs; too much drinking from being welded into your homes (and the Centers for Disease Control and Prevention (CDC) data now shows more deaths in the US from alcoholism than from Covid); and so on.

The deaths flowing *because of* lockdowns will outnumber the lives saved by lockdowns by an order of magnitude or more. And did readers know that Sweden, one country that did not lockdown but focused on protection of the old and vulnerable, now has pretty much the best European pandemic numbers going? I refer to excess deaths and Covid death rates and how Sweden is faring compared to other countries in Europe. Well, on the pandemic despotism front, again, Roskam and the IPA were there on the side of freedom.

Of course, there was also the Peter Ridd affair, which is why I have been invited to write this chapter, and of course I will be moving to that topic in a moment. But again, when it came to how an academic at James Cook University (JCU) was treated for speaking his mind about the GBR, well, the IPA was in Ridd's corner.

Now on all these issues I, personally, have been on same side as Roskam and the IPA. Writing, arguing, trying to defend free speech and freedom. But let us be honest, brutally honest. These are tough times for freedom. The current US President, Joe Biden, whether he knows it or not, is the least friendly president for free speech since President John Adams who pushed through the appalling Aliens and Sedition Act at the end of the 18th century.

And as for Australia – and I realise this might put off a few readers, but I am going to be bluntly honest all the same – the former Liberal prime minister was in the running to win the title of "Liberal PM with the least concern for free speech and freedom in the history of Australia". Heck, Mr Morrison seems to think concern about free speech (and I quote the man himself) "doesn't create one job, doesn't open one business, doesn't give anyone one extra hour (of work)". Plainly Mr Morrison does not understand how the West grew wealthy through the wide-open competition of ideas; he did not foresee the devastation (much of it economic) that the pandemic despotism would bring about, including cancelling and stifling people who were opposed to blanket lockdowns; and he never read Mark Steyn's claim "that everything is downstream of culture" – which it is. And I will not go into the proposal by the last Liberal government to give ACMA the power to be this country's thought-police. This was a Liberal government pushing censorship for heaven's sake!

So, yes, these are tough times to be free speech and freedom warriors. In all these instances I have mentioned, above, in which we have all been fighting the free-speech battle, it is not as though we have been winning all that much. Here and there a victory – the QUT students prevailed – but a lot more losses than wins. Ridd will attest to that, unfortunately. But we fighters know that this is a long-term game and what happens now, and the fight one shows now, builds the ground for what happens later. So we fight on. John Roskam and the IPA have been terrific warriors and it has been a pleasure to be associated with him and with the IPA.

Now my chapter is going to be somewhat meandering. For those of you of a certain age you may recall the wonderful and great broadcaster Alistair Cooke who for almost half a century delivered a weekly "Letter from America" on the World Service of the BBC. Cooke would start in one place with a simple message and then serpentine here, there, and everywhere, before finally arriving back where he started. Well, my chapter will aim to be a pale imitation of that sort of "Letter from America". I am going to start by giving you a sketch of today's Australian universities. (And if you went to university 25 or more years ago then you need to forget everything you think you know about university life; it is a different galaxy today.) After I have done that I am going to shift to consider the concept of academic freedom. Then, if any readers are still awake, I will have a few things to say about the High Court decision in the Ridd case. And I will link that to the freedom battle, which should just about bring us back to the start.

Before I give you a precis of what is wrong with today's universities – because these problems exist across the Anglosphere to varying degrees – let me paint you a picture from my university, The University of Queensland. It is a beautiful campus with an Oxbridge-like quadrangle amidst the oldest buildings, and that is where my law school is situated.

And by the way, my University of Queensland law school is, in my view, by far the most conservative law school in Australia. We have about 40 faculty members. Of those 40 about seven or eight would normally vote Coalition. The other 32 would vote Green or Labor. Now I am not joking when I say that that makes us by far – by far – the most conservative law school in the country. I have heard us described as a far-right law school or heavily conservative law school – and I immodestly think I may be partly to blame for that – but that critique occurs in the context of a law school where 80 per cent of the law professors and lecturers vote Left. If you think that is a bad omen as regards viewpoint diversity on today's Aussie campuses, well, you are right.

But some days, mid-morning, I venture out with colleagues for a coffee or tea at the Merlo's coffee shop in the quadrangle. It is the busiest Merlo's in Brisbane. Academics often tell you they work hard. I spent a few years working as a litigator in a big Toronto law firm and at the Bar in London. I can assure you that they do not. Heck, I don't. But we wander down to this Merlo's. Some of the patrons will order their half-macchiato with soya milk; others will take their decaf flat whites on almond milk; you will notice people asking for cappuccinos on oat milk – because they have discovered that almonds use up too much water to grow. Taking regular milk, as I do, is very much a minority taste and a way to garner judgemental stares. Every second person has a nut allergy. Gluten-free brownies are the order of the day. Lots and lots of customers, unbelievably, will still be wearing masks. In short, this is the home of the fair-dinkum Aussie battler; it is where you will find Australia's median voter. Okay, maybe not. Australian campuses line up with the opinions of Twitter far more than they do with any constituency in the country that does not have a Green Party MP.

Now if you look at US data, where donations to political parties are public information, it is plain that there has been a near total collapse of viewpoint diversity on campus. Fifty years ago it might have been four Democrats for each Republican on campus. Now it will be 15:1 or worse. US law schools have almost that sort of ratio. In some university departments (think gender studies, indigenous studies, sociology and even political science) the number of conservative academics rhymes with the fifth Roman Emperor, the pyromaniac. And Jonathan Haidt, a left-of-centre US academic who laments the collapse of conservatives on campus, details this chapter and verse. In my view, it is pretty much the same here in Australia. Harder to prove, but the same.

Partly this is driven by concerns for "diversity", which means diversity of reproductive organs and of skin pigmentation on campus. And that means identity politics because what you do as part of each university's huge diversity bureaucracy is you start with some desirable job or student place – it is never an undesirable or a dangerous job – and you look first at the overall percentage of the population of some group (women, Aborigines, gays, whatever) and then you look at the percentage of those groups in the desirable jobs or places (never the undesirable, dangerous ones, remember). And any mismatch has to be – is deemed to be – discrimination. It is never put down to individuals' differing preferences, or life aspirations, or abilities. So this "group thinking" or "statistical thinking" forces everything into a sort of tribalism and then it imposes a quiet, implicit quota. Diversity bureaucracies create a monolithic orthodoxy on campus (and in the corporate boardroom and everywhere) because those who disagree are not promoted, or they are slowly forced out, or they so dislike the corporate culture they quit.

Take me. I could never be a dean of law or hold any higher position in an Australian university. (Not that I would want one. I don't. However, I am making a point here.) First off, I would never go through the charade of the "acknowledgement of country" that begins everything on campus (soon they will probably do one before you order coffee at Merlo's). I think these ritualistic utterings are condescending; they are patronising; they are incoherent; and they are straight-out virtue-signalling. Those who mouth them never go to an outback Aboriginal community to help out, or spend time helping brutalised young girls, or give up their jobs to Aborigines, or hand their homes over because they actually (not pretend, but actually) think those homes of theirs are on stolen land. No, those who utter these things are merely showing that they are part of today's moral elect. It is like a modern-day version of the Anglicans' 39 Articles that you had to pretend to agree with to go to Oxford or Cambridge in the 1800s.

Likewise, I would never agree to administer any sort of quotas or affirmative action programs, which permeate our universities and are what "diversity" and "equity" are all about. So I simply could not get these higher-up university administrative jobs. Nor could many other conservatives. As it happens, you almost certainly *could* refuse to stand for the national anthem, or say that James Cook launched Invasion Day and that would not stop you at all from getting these jobs.

Think back to when former Chief Justice French of the High Court conducted his report into free speech on campus – and why do the Coalition governments, when looking into problems on campus, always talk to vice-chancellors (who are part of the problem and who as a caste are no friends to conservatives) and seek out Labor-appointed top judges (or any sort of judge who has not set foot on a university campus in decades, save perhaps to give a speech to judge-adoring law students) but never talk to any of the dwindling number of actual conservatives on campus? (There have been more than a couple of recent books edited by conservatives on the problems with our universities and these and their authors have been completely ignored by Coalition ministers.[1])

Well, Mr French looked at universities' codes of conduct (he read the papers) and he looked at cases of these codes being weaponised and concluded that, all in all, there is no free-speech problem at Australian universities. But this conclusion overlooks the fact that when 90 to 95 per cent of academics (and a higher percentage of university administrators) are "lefties" – I use the well-known term of art here to encompass all those who share the progressive, woke worldview – then those people truly can say anything they want. There is no free-speech problem for lefties in today's universities, none at all. So in that statistical sense Mr French is certainly correct.

The second, related, error is to overlook the fact that these codes of conduct are discretionarily enforced. They do not enforce themselves. It is up to the vice-chancellor whether to invoke one in order to discipline someone. And it is hard to think of what sort of thing an academic on the political Left could say or do that would push a university administrator into using the code of conduct against him or her. Remember, the top university administrators agree with this person's "progressive" worldview, or in fact probably hold it even more strongly. Hence maybe, just maybe, if the academic on the Left were egregiously vicious about Israel, the code of conduct might be invoked. But that is it; that is the only possibility I can think of. Meantime, and though there are few cases, when we do see cases where the code of conduct is invoked it is in fact against non-progressives, against the sceptics, and against the iconoclasts on campus (which, today, overwhelmingly means the conservatives).

The other point about today's universities, and this point unexpectedly happens to unite the Left and the Right on campus, is that Australian universities are the most bureaucratic in the Anglosphere. Well over 50 per cent of employees are administrators – they do not teach and they do not publish. They are internal rent-seekers. Would any reader run a business that way? Our top university administrators are among the highest paid in the world. Many vice-chancellors get $1.3 million a year, or more in the G-8 universities. They employ massive diversity bureaucracies. If everyone so employed failed to turn up for work for a year, the university would work just as well. No, it would do better. (And for what it is worth, that is one of the definitions of a "bullshit" job, that not having it in place makes things no worse or better.)

When I worked in New Zealand at the Otago law school in Dunedin, our law faculty would have meetings where we debated things and then voted whether to do it or not. In my 17 years in Australia – and I am not exaggerating here for effect, I mean this literally – there has never once been a single matter of substance that our law school got to vote on, not once. And, again, I am being dead serious about that. Everything is imposed from above. Seriously, Australia's model for universities lies somewhere between the former East German economic model and the General Motors of the 1950s corporate model. Everything is top-down and *uber*-centralised. Oh, and they have made "grant getting" a proxy for quality. So you have this huge grant-getting internal university bureaucracy – not to mention the huge government grant-giving bureaucracy in Canberra – and both need to be fed. Universities pay a lot of administrators a lot of money to oversee this grant-getting machine.

In the hard sciences this sort of makes sense, sort of, maybe. But in law, the humanities, and the social sciences most academics can publish without any big government grants or any grants at all (and I remain a virgin on that score); these academics do not need any sort of grant to do their job perfectly well. In fact, often it turns out that they have to sit down and try to dream up things that will allow them to apply for grant money. And here is the thing. If you take two academics and assume that each is otherwise equal. They both publish an article in a worldwide top journal – let us take law and say they publish in the *Oxford Journal of Legal Studies* or the *Harvard Law Review*. Professor X wrote his by thinking, reading, going to the library, but with no grant money. Professor Y got a huge Australian Research Council (ARC) grant to publish in exactly the same journal. You know what? Professor Y will be lauded by the university; she will be promoted; she will be deemed wonderful. By contrast, Professor X will not be promoted and he may well be fired down the road. Think about it.

Two equal outcomes but the one who needs millions of dollars of extra taxpayer support is feted. Would you buy a car based on the company that got the most government aid? (By the way, notice that I did not use renewable electricity for my rhetorical question example. I leave readers to work out why.)

And so there is this huge grant-getting bureaucracy on campus that needs to be fed, hence it takes a big cut out of all grants won. I have been arguing for 15 years that a Coalition government should eliminate all grants and or at least get rid of the need for grant getting everywhere outside the hard sciences and medicine. No one listens to me, though, but I believe it would make an immediate improvement on campus.

But now take this need to get grants and move to the social sciences and imagine you are a conservative academic. Do you think those who award grants will fund someone in favour of stopping the boats? In favour of traditional marriage? Against renewables? Anyone who disliked the Covid despotism and saw it as the greatest inroads on our civil liberties in three centuries (like me, say)? Or anything with a remotely right-of-centre outlook? But if you do not get grants you probably do not get promoted, or maybe retained. So ask yourself again why viewpoint diversity on campus has collapsed and why conservative professors like me are so few that it is too risky for us to travel together on the same plane.

Let me put this all succinctly in these terms. Australian universities are worse now, today, than they were nine years ago when the Coalition came to power in 2013 – more bureaucratic, fewer conservative academics, far more woke and politically correct, lots of grade inflation, lower standards, more affirmative action and a massive "diversity" bureaucracy. All brought to you while Liberal ministers were in office if we are being honest.

That, at any rate, is a brief overview of Australian universities to set the scene for you. Now let me turn to the notion or concept or theory of academic freedom. There is quite a bit of literature on this in the US. I am just going to touch on the basics. What is it about being a university academic that produces a tenable claim that he or she ought to have a freedom not possessed by others? There are various schools of thought but here are the two biggest and most plausible:

1. the "serving the common good" or "critic and conscience of society" conception;

2. the "it's just a job" conception.

The first one is commonly trotted out. Personally, I think it is laughable. I made that point 20 years ago in New Zealand in a newspaper piece. It didn't win me any friends on campus but anyone who thinks university academics, as a group, can plausibly be thought of as "the critic and conscience of society" or as "serving the common good" needs to spend more time at a university.

Far more plausible is the second one I noted, the "it's just a job" understanding of academic freedom. On this view, academic freedom is not an off-shoot or corollary of some natural right or some fundamental entitlement to free speech. To be clear, it is *not* a sub-branch of free-speech thinking. Rather, it is nothing more nor less than a freedom to do the job passingly well, and one that rests on nothing more than the good long-term consequences that flow from upholding it. So academic freedom is a freedom from the fear of job reprisals in the context of functioning as an academic.

If one is following arguments and evidence where they lead – without regard to whether they will support one's political goals or enhance one's popularity – that freedom, the freedom to do that, is what academic freedom protects. Or should protect. Why should it? Because in the long-term doing so will deliver benefits for the society that is paying the way for academics and universities. And by the way, this is no direct sort of consequentialism where governments pick winners. Australian governments do that, but it is a mug's game.

Instead, what I am defending is the indirect pursuit of good long-term consequences. It is not achieved when academics aim directly at creating more wealth for society, or at producing valuable goods for society. Yes, ultimately that production is why taxpayers are prepared to pay for relatively privileged and cocooned academics. But those academics do not deliver when academic inquiry is guided by directly aiming for these goods. They best produce these valuable goods (and by 'valuable goods' I include the passing on of cultural knowledge when history or English or philosophy *et al.* are taught properly) when academics are *not* guided by the aim of directly producing them, but rather by aiming to follow arguments where they lead. Put simply, these academics aim for the truth. The benefits for everyone else are by-products of that.

Outside of doing the job, academics have no more freedom or free-speech protection than anyone else. They get, or should get, only what is needed to do the job – and we should not get all starry eyed and think many or most of them are doing anything remotely open to being characterised as "upholding the common good" or "being the critic and conscience of society". It is a job, and outside of that job academics are just regular employees. There are no special employee privileges for academics outside of that, at least in my view. It is the freedom to do one's job and it is limited to academic matters.

Of course, part of that is the freedom from the fear of job reprisals for doing the job of seeking the truth. So that is the question when we turn to the saga of Peter Ridd. Can we understand what happened in terms of Peter's "just doing his job", remembering that doing that carries with it a freedom from the fear of job reprisals? Or, was his firing just part and parcel of any regular employee process – such as when an employee is disciplined for infringing copyright; for stealing; for insubordination; for having sex with minors; for defaming someone; for not turning up to work; and the like.

My view is that the High Court of Australia got it badly wrong, and that Ridd was dealt a bad result. His academic freedom *was* infringed. In the result the High Court only managed to virtue-signal – that is to tell us all how important academic freedom was in the abstract and how much they, these top judges, valued it when it did not matter to the result. But when it did matter the top judges preferred the JCU code of conduct and the acceptability of the university's reprisals against Ridd for his having done his job the way it is supposed to be done. I would characterise it as the High Court, in practice, selling academic freedom down the river.

I am not going to run everyone through a dry analysis of what I take the High Court's reasoning to be in the Ridd case. I set out my basic take on the case in the pages of the *Spectator Australia* back in late October 2021.[2] The gist of my take is that the *Ridd* case is bifurcated. In one part the top judges tell us how important academic (or as it is put in the case, intellectual) freedom is. That is mentioned in Clause 14 of the Enterprise Agreement (enterprise agreement). And the judges tell us that it trumps the university's code of conduct's "play nice" diktats. But then when it does matter, when it really matters in practice – as regards whether Peter can be fired or not based on the university's confidentiality requirements as regards its disciplinary proceedings – the High Court gives an emphatic win to JCU. Get this. The judges say the initial university disciplining of Ridd (for what he said about the Barrier Reef and about his colleagues) was wholly unwarranted. They side with Ridd. The original 2016 censure should not have been handed out. However, the later 'final' censure and then the termination were justified, said the High Court. Why? Because according to the court academic freedom does *not* extend as far as protecting an academic who openly protests against the way the university is running its disciplinary proceedings against him (because that breaches the confidentiality requirement). In my view, freedom from the fear of job reprisals should be made of sterner stuff. Or put differently, if the confidentiality requirement can protect proceedings that the judges say should never have been instituted in the first place – if that and that alone trumps academic freedom – then it is a pretty hollow freedom that really does not allow the Ridds of the world to do their jobs and pursue the truth where they see it. Here is part of how I put it in the *Spectator Australia*:[3]

> [The High Court of Australia view] amounts to this prescription to all academics: if your university wrongfully tries to silence you when you speak out and it wrongfully takes disciplinary proceedings against you, you just have to be a good little boy. No rising to the JCU bait. No talking to anyone about what's happening to you. Just go through the university disciplinary proceedings and trust them and the people who screwed you over in the first place.

> How do you raise money to contest those proceedings if, like me, you're not in the union and you can't tell anyone about them? Details my friend. Just bask in the warm knowledge that at some point down the road, after suffering through the university's proceedings,

you will be able to engage a top KC, bring judicial review proceedings, and then all can become public. It reminds one of Anatole France's line that "the law, in its majestic equality, forbids the rich as well as the poor to sleep under bridges".

If by fluke you're a multi-millionaire academic (like our world's highest paid vice-chancellors) the practical effects of this ruling won't bother you too much. For all other academics it will have a significant chilling effect. No matter how disgracefully you are treated there is no going nuclear says our High Court. (Full disclosure: had I been treated the way Ridd was after voicing his views about the Reef I'd have had an op-ed out the next day about the disciplinary process, and now be out of a job.) Still, the court's advice is to trust the university process for a few years, without telling anyone, and all will be well (if you manage to afford a lawyer and win your eventual judicial review action). Or, as Mark Steyn regularly comments, maybe "the process in these sort of things *is* the punishment" and so most academics (not being hot-heads like me) will just weigh things up and opt to keep their controversial views to themselves ... What do you think is likely to be the response to this decision by most academics? I work with them. Bravery is not the most notable virtue of academia.

It gets worse of course. That's because if we leave aside actual criminal behaviour (which is covered by the code of conduct and in that realm is uncontentious) and focus on the expression of views, the background truth of the matter that no judge dared mention is that universities across the Anglosphere are today places of monolithic orthodoxy. Untold studies have shown that conservative viewpoints on campus have collapsed in the last half century and are today the equivalent of endangered species ... For 90 per cent of academics subscribing to the usual left-leaning pieties it is hard to imagine a university anywhere in this country invoking the code of conduct against them. For them there is no free-speech problem – which is why Robert French's claim is true in a technical sense, but only in that sense. You have to be an outlier, an iconoclast, a dissenter, or yes a conservative – maybe a global warming sceptic, a transgender sceptic, against lockdowns, someone who is against "the Voice", etc, – and then we can imagine the code being invoked. But that's precisely when academic freedom is supposed to come to the aid of the unorthodox viewpoint.

Alas, according to the High Court in *Ridd* this intellectual freedom guarantee can let you speak to start. But when the university opts to come after you for doing so, you have to be a good little boy. Keep shtum! Trust the process. But the point is that Ridd didn't trust the process. I wouldn't have either. Justice Rangiah in dissent in the Federal Court, described the university's confidentiality process that the majority of the Federal Court (and now the High Court) said you had to succumb to "a Kafkaesque scenario of a person secretly accused and secretly found guilty of a disciplinary offence but unable to reveal, under threat of further secret charges being brought, that he or she had ever been charged and found guilty". Nowhere did the High Court say that Rangiah's characterisation of the proceedings was wrong; only that Ridd should have meekly submitted to them. Heck, at one point Ridd was told he couldn't even tell his wife what was happening.

In a sentence, the High Court said an academic could *not* be punished for speaking, but could be punished for complaining about being punished for what we now are told he could rightfully say in the first place. Got that?

To me that delivers no protection against the fear of job reprisals when "you're just doing your job". The breach of confidentiality is made separate from the original university wrongdoing in the 2016 and 2017 wrongful censures. That is nowhere dictated in the enterprise agreement. It was the pettifogging, academic freedom-enervating choice. Nor did this result have anything to do with the way the Ridd legal team argued the case – the suggestion of which by the judges being pure misdirection and trying to shift the blame from their own enervated understanding of academic freedom's aegis. Both the Ridd side and the university side argued the whole "18 pieces of alleged misconduct" were a package, an all-or-nothing matter. Ridd said they all related to academic freedom. JCU said that none did. Yet the judges said, in effect, that the onus was on Ridd to make out every single element or lose the "all-or-nothing" bet; it was not on the university to do this.

This is the most hollow understanding of academic freedom going. At some point Ridd needed academic freedom to be deemed to encompass not having to meekly submit to the Kafkaesque (Justice Rangiah's words, not mine) disciplinary proceedings, with their incredibly onerous confidentiality requirements. Heck, the High Court even half-cheated by using as an example of the importance of not breaching confidentiality, the case of naming another individual involved. But Ridd had never done that, so the suggestion or analogy was inapt. Or flat out misleading.

All in all, this was not the High Court's finest hour. It was a pretty insipid and lousy decision in my view. Its effect amounted to another chink being taken out of the armour of freedom in this country. But again, the IPA was there fighting all the way. There is no organisation in this country that has done more for freedom.

And that takes us back, full circle and Alistair Cooke-like, to where I started. Hence, I will end this chapter and stop now. Let me again just thank John Roskam and the entire IPA team for having invited me to contribute this chapter.

---

1   The best one to look at is the one edited by William Coleman. See William Coleman (ed.), Campus Meltdown: The Deepening Crisis in Australian Universities (Connor Court Publishing, 2019). The book has a tremendous array of authors, from Australia and around the world, advancing not just diagnoses but prescriptions for improvement and the reception from Liberal politicians has been crickets. Zero. Nada. Nothing. They prefer to chat to vice-chancellors who, frankly, are part of the problem.

2   J Allan, 'They Ridd us of that turbulent academic' Spectator Australia (23 October 2021).

3   Ibid.

A cascade of injustice: A critical review of the Ridd case

Aynsley Kellow

—

It is as fatal as it is cowardly to blink facts because they are not to our taste. John Tyndall, 1877.

The High Court's rejection of Peter Ridd's appeal against his dismissal represents the end point of a cascade of injustice, not just against Ridd himself, but against the basic principles of scientific endeavour, and thus the public who depend upon the best possible science to inform the discourses that support the best public policy.

In this chapter, I reflect briefly on the court's decision, though I leave a detailed critique of its legal reasoning to others. I provide a detailed examination of the nature of science and the conduct of science relating to the GBR, concluding that Ridd's criticism about the poor quality assurance (QA) underlying that science should have been supported and acted upon, rather than suppressed. James Cook University (JCU) clearly has issues that Ridd was justified in highlighting, as subsequent science has shown. Rather than suppress Ridd's call to arms, it might have acted as Deakin University did in the Briggs case and helped remedy what appears to be (in the conclusion of a report into one JCU case) a culture of poor research practice at best.

Science, law and expertise

The decision of the High Court in *Ridd v James Cook University* [2021] HCA 32 was passing strange. The court held that Ridd should not have been subject to censure by JCU for publicly highlighting QA problems with science on the GBR. The learned justices even gave a lengthy disquisition on the nature and importance of academic freedom. But it went on to uphold the subsequent censures and ultimate dismissal of Ridd for breaching JCU's directions (including one that forbade satire and parody) that he should refrain from comment about his censure as this breached the Enterprise Agreement (enterprise agreement) (see Appendix A).

Ridd, it would seem, was wrongly censured, but his sin was to complain publicly about that wrongful censure. This is beyond satire and parody. Given the wrongfulness of the censure, why should he not complain about it?

The court relied on a line of reasoning that, while Ridd's comments for which he was censured lay within his disciplinary expertise, his public comments about the suppression of such views did not, and were therefore not covered by the notion of academic freedom.

The High Court, by this logic, would have supported the suppression of the research on intelligence by James R. Flynn.[1] Flynn was an ethical philosopher who sought to rebut Arthur Jensen's research on race and intelligence in a few pages for a book on the justification of humane ideals. Finding nothing but *ad hominem* attacks, Flynn embarked on his own research and upturned the field of educational psychology, discovering what became known as the Flynn Effect: that performance by all on intelligence tests improved throughout the 20th Century. (The experts in the field had missed this because they customarily dealt only with standardised data.) The High Court would have upheld the suppression of Flynn's research, because it lay outside his area of expertise.

I would also maintain, however, that the philosophy of science and a critical awareness of the faults in the conduct of scientific research should lie within the expertise of *any* scientist, including that at their own institution. Unfortunately, the scientific method does not appear to be part of the curriculum for science courses, even for scientists undertaking research for higher degrees. The result is that we have the replication crisis that Ridd identified, citing the work of John Ioannidis, who has found that about half of medical science papers are wrong.[2] The result in climate science is that model results are presented as data, and the word "could" appears frequently in scientific papers that contain conjectures, but rarely any attempts at refutations.

The court might have reflected on the point that it should be within the expertise of *every* scientist to address the integrity of the scientific process, even though the philosophy of science appears to have been a huge omission from the education of the present generation of scientists. They might have noted that the beginnings of the Enlightenment lay, *inter alia*, with Galileo, not just with his contribution to astronomy, but with that to the principles of scientific enquiry in the face of the powerful forces of the institutions (represented by the Roman Inquisition) that imposed metaphysical constraints on the development of what should have been empirical propositions, or what Ayer termed "synthetic propositions".[3] *All* scientists should be deemed to have expertise concerning the proper conduct of science, and in the view of this author the High Court erred in this regard in its ruling by expecting Ridd to suffer an injustice in silence. As his views were later published in the scientific literature, they would almost certainly qualify him as being an expert witness under the *Daubert* decision laid down by the US Supreme Court.[4]

The decision in *Daubert* is helpful, because it points us to what constitutes "science" – usually taken to mean something like "disciplined knowledge". The work of Karl Popper[5] points us in a useful direction, insisting that science consists of the generation of hypotheses that must be capable of being falsified by observation, and that we should accept their validity only conditionally, fully expecting that they might be falsified by future observations. We accept hypotheses only conditionally and have greater faith in those that have survived repeated attempts at falsification. (As Thomas Kuhn noted,[6] the advancement of knowledge often moves in "paradigm shifts" as older truths collapse, and as Paul Feyerabend observed, contests between scientists do not always follow Marquess of Queensberry Rules.[7])

While Popper's prescriptive advice is sound, it is confronted by several obstacles as contemporary science is practised, not least that negative results or falsification bring little kudos. This is reflected in the difficulty in getting negative results published, although the problem has begun to be recognised; Murudkar has identified 10 journals devoted to publishing negative results,[8] including the *Journal of Negative Results*, although one she listed, the *Journal of Negative Results in Biomedicine*, ceased publication in 2017.

The High Court's largest error, in my view, was that it took an unnecessarily narrow view of "political communication", which it had previously found was an implied right that should not be limited by executives or legislatures. But politics is not limited to the electoral process; communication that informs the development of public policy is also "political communication". The court did not need to stretch its thoughts too far to strike down those provisions of the JCU's enterprise agreement under the *Fair Work Act* on the grounds that these limited Ridd's ability to communicate JCU's attempt to limit him conveying problems with the quality of science, which in turn was informing public policy on the GBR.

Science on the Great Barrier Reef

The GBR is an iconic marvel, and we are understandably concerned when the corals that are the essential life forms on which it depends suffer from some kind of degradation. It has come under attack from crown-of-thorns starfish. It has been threatened by bleaching from periodic El Niños conveniently attributed to climate change,[9] as if the El Niño–Southern Oscillation (ENSO) wouldn't exist without the forcing by increased carbon dioxide and other greenhouse gases released since the onset of the Industrial Revolution. Literature tends to show an absence of bleaching before 1980, and of crown-of-thorns starfish infestations before 1960.[10] Tim Blair once set out the history of claims of doom for the reef, with the historical record suggesting the doom portended for it in news reports dated back to an ALP state election campaign in 1969, but there is evidence of both bleaching and crown-of-thorns well before then.[11]

Now, we are told, there is a new threat from agricultural run-off, especially as it contains silt and agricultural chemicals. It is important to note that Ridd and colleagues have shown just how unlikely this latest threat is, demonstrating that the reef is flushed daily by tides and currents that dwarf the annual flow from coastal rivers that have many kilometres to travel to reach the reef in most places.[12]

The reef has proven to be a lucrative source of research funding for scientists studying it, and this has been enhanced by the threat posed by climate change. There is a kind of implicit "give us some research funding, or the reef gets it". Millions of dollars are at stake, and Ridd's sin was to threaten that funding. The size of the cash flow is staggering. The Turnbull government notoriously granted $444 million in April 2018 to the Great Barrier Reef Foundation (GBRF), a charity that at the time had annual revenue of only about $10 million and employed just six full-time staff – a donation that came in for criticism by the Auditor-General. (The GBRF is well connected with reef scientists at both JCU and The University of Queensland, it should be noted.) The Commonwealth government allocated another $1 billion for GBR marine science in the 2022 Budget, and the new ALP government has promised another $220 million.

These are not trivial sums, and they are justified on the basis of the natural wonder of a World Heritage listed treasure – and, of course, the negative impact on reef-based tourism in the region where there is bleaching. I observed in my 2007 book *Science and Public Policy: The Virtuous Corruption of Virtual Environmental Science*[13] that the noble cause of environmental protection often placed what Iain Boal[14] called a "value slope" across the conduct of environmental science – especially when it was based primarily upon computer models, rather than observational science. I distinguished then such corruption of scientific process from corruption by venal causes, such as the influence of large sums of money, but with reef science both influences are present: a noble cause reinforced by the presence of large sums of money in what Bruce Yandle called a "Bootlegger and Baptist Coalition".[15] Such coalitions are extremely powerful.

Changing nature, changing reef

I want to suggest, however, that – while noble – the cause of "saving" the GBR is a lost one. The reef, like nature itself, has never existed in harmonious balance but for anthropogenic factors – especially anthropogenic climate change for which the reef has been used as a convenient harbinger in recent years.

My reason for making this statement is that ecological science acknowledges that nature is replete with change and perturbation, which is certainly the case with the GBR, and we cannot accept a conception of the reef as existing in some kind of delicate, harmonious balance, although many try. For example, a JCU document states "tourists flocked to visit the reef, upsetting its delicate ecological equilibrium".[16] Any deleterious change is thus attributed to human agency, and "political ecology" maintains that view.[17] Many scientists and activists came to see tourism as a threat to the reef,[18] so are perhaps indifferent to the negative effect of tales of "death of the reef" on tourism.

Environmental activists revere the idea of the "ancient" reef. Perhaps the most telling example came from journalist Rowan Jacobsen, who, in an "obituary" in *Outside* in October 2016 that went viral, dated the GBR to 25 million years BC.[19] While many news sources repeated this nonsense, it was in *The Guardian,* not usually noted for its restraint on environmental matters, that it was suggested the GBR was not dead yet, and described Jacobsen as a "food and travel writer".[20] Yet it allowed the age of 25 million years to stand unchecked, as did the then (and recently retired) Director of the ARC Centre of Excellence for Coral Reef Studies (CECRS), based at JCU, Terry Hughes.[21]

But the reef is, in fact, a relatively recent structure geologically, thought to have commenced developing on an older platform only some 20,000 years before the present day, at the time of the Last Glacial Maximum when sea levels were 120 metres below the present. Both the Great Barrier Reef Marine Park Authority and the Australian Institute of Marine Science (AIMS) agree on this.[22] The sea level evened out relatively recently, about 6,000 years ago, which amounts to the blink of an eye in geological terms, but it is not tenable to assume that the reef has been stable since, except for damage inflicted by humanity. At a very fundamental level, of course, continental drift tells us that Australia continues to move northwards at a rate of about seven centimetres per year. It seems reasonable to expect that the reef will continue to change in response to such geological shifts and the variability imposed by ENSO phases.

While episodes of coral bleaching are undoubtedly bad news for tourism operators plying their trade adjacent to the bleaching, bleaching appears in fact to be the mechanism whereby corals adapt to gently warming water, expelling the zooxanthellae that provide them with sustenance, but then taking in new organisms. One could be forgiven for thinking that warming temperatures are the sole and recently developed cause of coral bleaching, and yet the history of science on the matter suggests otherwise.

The history of the science on coral bleaching is interesting, because the attribution of bleaching predominantly to climate change is relatively recent, and it has made a convenient canvas on which to depict the climate change issue, especially since the 1998 mass bleaching event. Prior to this, climate change barely rates a mention in the literature, with changes in osmotic pressure from high run-off after hurricanes affecting salinity, siltation, and so on, being regarded as the causes.[23] Even Hughes in 1994 attributed the decline in reefs in Jamaica to the effects of overfishing, hurricane damage, and disease. Hughes did discuss hurricanes, and thus weather, as a factor, but did so in non-catastrophic terms:

Hurricanes, typhoons, or cyclones are predictable, recurrent events and an integral part of the natural dynamics of a coral reef. The regeneration of a healthy reef system is facilitated by rapid colonization of larval recruits ...[24]

In arguing for the pre-eminence of climate change, Hoegh-Guldberg, University of Queensland member of the CECRS , showed that the bleaching events since 1979 seemed to be related to El Niño events,[25] but this rather detracted from his "climate change" theme, because such events are thought to have occurred every two to seven years for the past 300 years – well before the industrial era. The inconvenient notion that bleaching might have occurred regularly before there was anthropogenic global warming was reported by Kamenos and Hennige,[26] but this was quickly countered with a paper by Hoegh-Guldberg et al,[27] which, ironically, questioned the reliability of the historical temperature record that forms the basis of the global temperature records for the 70 per cent of the Earth's surface that is covered by water. Hoegh-Guldberg et al stated that they had been instrumental in rejecting the Kamenos and Hennige paper several times previously, which is reminiscent of an email from Phil Jones to Michael Mann revealed by the Climategate scandal: "I can't see either of these papers being in the next IPCC report. Kevin and I will keep them out somehow – even if we have to redefine what the peer-review literature is!" Or a referee's reason for rejecting a paper by Garth Paltridge, former Chief Atmospheric Scientist at CSIRO, that undermined the assumed positive feedback from water vapour: "the only object I can see for this paper is for the authors to get something in the peer-reviewed literature which the ignorant can cite as supporting lower climate sensitivity than the standard IPCC range."[28]

But Hoegh-Guldberg et al simply ignored observational evidence that coral bleaching is not just a recent phenomenon. In evidence from the 1928–29 GBR expedition, led by Charles Yonge, Yonge observed:

> By heating for an appropriate time at certain temperatures, it is possible to kill many of the algae without damaging the coral; this occurred naturally on many parts of the reef flat during the low tides in the summer.[29]

The JCU Library has a Sir Charles Maurice Yonge Collection, and there is even a reef named for him, so one might expect that there would be some awareness of his contribution. There is a five-part series by the JCU Library on the expedition of 1928–29,[30] but that too makes no mention of his observations of summer bleaching. Interestingly, Goreau mentions Yonge's observations of bleaching.[31] Hoegh-Guldberg, cites Goreau, and therefore has no reason not to be aware of Yonge's observations.[32]

It seems earlier evidence of bleaching has been largely ignored by those associated with the CECRS. It is possible Hoegh-Guldberg is simply incurious, but he certainly provides evidence of Boal's "value slope" that conduces towards certain forms of consciousness. What is certain is that Hoegh-Guldberg, with a Greenpeace connection, provides a critical case study that invalidates the claim of Schaffelke et al in response to a paper by Larcombe and Ridd that there is no connection between science and politics, and does so on the science of the GBR.

There are two avenues for the corruption of "science as process" and the triumph of "science as institution" – and an authoritative institution at that. One is the commitment to a noble cause, such as saving the planet. This is rarely patently on display, as while researchers are today required to disclose any conflicts of interest when publishing, they are not required to disclose commitments to political causes. This can occasionally be seen, as was the case with Hoegh-Guldberg's paper predicting widespread future bleaching of coral reefs published in 1999. Hoegh-Guldberg predicted that most coral reef systems would experience near-annual bleaching events exceeding the extent of the 1998 bleaching event by 2040, and some coral reefs would reach this point by 2020.[33] We can mark that down as a failed prediction.

Larcombe and Ridd

Together with Piers Larcombe, Ridd repeated his call for better QA on GBR science in *Marine Pollution Bulletin* in 2018.[34] Larcombe and Ridd argued in depth for the criticisms Ridd had made in 2015, pointing to the need for better QA in science when it was being used to inform public policy and spend public money – what they termed "policy-science". They advocated for a new institution to undertake quality reviews and audits of important scientific research underpinning government spending decisions on the environment – an "Institute for Policy-Science Quality Control" (IPSQC).

Schaffelke et al questioned "the value and validity of Larcombe and Ridd's proposed concept of 'policy-science', as it disregards the boundary that separates science and policy".[35] They argued that scientific studies were conducted on their scientific merit, and that science used to inform policies was no different from any other scientific research. They argued that Larcombe and Ridd's argument could lead to "indiscriminately questioning the rigour of any science that underpinned policies". Among the examples of policies underpinned by such science they named the Montreal

Protocol, research on the toxicology of pharmaceuticals, and the Stockholm on Persistent Organic Pollutants, and "research identifying the emission of greenhouse gases as the dominant cause of observed warming (that underpins the climate change policies of many nations, including the Paris agreement)". The recent book by Steven Koonin would suggest climate policies are based on a misrepresentation of science underlying governments' understanding of climate science.[36]

The notion that the science surrounding a nonlinear coupled ocean–atmosphere system should be protected from "indiscriminate questioning" is risible, and they seem ignorant of the fact that the testing of pharmaceuticals and pesticides is governed by the very kinds of regulatory regime that Larcombe and Ridd were advocating. These include the OECD Guidelines on Good Laboratory Practice and Mutual Acceptance of Data, and national regulatory policies that include audit and accreditation of testing laboratories. And it is politics, not science, that has inhibited the reframing of the regulation of toxic substances based on the outmoded linear non-threshold model that fails to take into account the contemporary findings of hormesis.[37] Instead, regulatory policies are more costly than they need be as they strive for elusive and counterproductive purity.

Schaffelke et al cited a rather curious authority for their understanding of the scientific method: not a book or paper from the philosophy of science literature, but a post by Michael Grubb.[38] The post was published on *The Conversation,* a blog that has an editorial policy of censoring any "climate denier" viewpoints, and which is (to their shame) funded by various universities. Grubb's complaint was that a paper he and his co-authors had published "concluded that there was more headroom than many had assumed before we breach the goals of the Paris Agreement". His problem was that a "far-right website" and the "more rabid elements in the media" had taken their research and used it to argue that action on climate change was less urgent.

This hardly helped the argument of Schaffelke et al, that there was a clear separation between science and policy. Here was Grubb complaining about the political interpretation of science. But the conflation of science and policy was even greater than that. Grubb now holds an academic post, but he was formerly employed by the environment group World Wildlife Fund (WWF) and continued as an academic to campaign for WWF and write letters and sign statements supporting climate action to the likes of the European Commission and the Scottish government.[39] Grubb was one of those who joined the pile-on in reviewing Björn Lomborg's *The Sceptical Environmentalist*. Grubb's review was better than many, but he mistakenly criticised Lomborg for attributing Britain's air quality improvements to technological change, rather than the *Clean Air Act 1956*. In fact, there is sound evidence that Lomborg was correct.[40] (Ironically, Grubb falsely claimed that Lomborg did not provide evidence for his statement – while providing no evidence for his own assertion.)

It might be objected that Grubb is just a social scientist and not a researcher working on the GBR, but there was a close relationship between science and politics in an article by Hoegh-Guldberg,[41] a prominent member of the CECRS – one of the first to create alarm over coral bleaching by linking it to climate change after the mass bleaching event of 1998, and pointing to six bleaching events since 1979, when effective observation seems to have commenced. His paper shows the weakness of the claim of Schaffelke et al that science (and reef science at that) is divorced from politics. What was interesting with the paper was that Hoegh-Guldberg acknowledged the assistance of Greenpeace International and three Greenpeace campaigners (Erwin Jackson, Bill Hare, and Gareth Walton) for "discussion and input at various points in the manuscript" – though the Greenpeace connection of the three was not made explicit. It would have been a great surprise if Hoegh-Guldberg concluded that climate change did *not* pose a threat to coral reefs.

The evidence supports Ridd's critique

Larcombe and Ridd listed eight papers that they considered pointed to a need for better QA processes with GBR science, providing a brief critique of each.[42] These were responded to by some GBR scientists in Schaffelke et al.[43] I do not wish here to adjudicate the merits of the claims or the rejoinders, but a more recent publication controversy does tend to suggest that Larcombe and Ridd have a point. Moreover, the report in *Science* drawing attention to poor quality research in the period before Ridd made the call for which he was censured is also linked to a scientific fraud committed by a JCU PhD graduate that was uncovered in Sweden.[44]

A 2020 paper by Clark et al published in *Nature* placed under suspicion dozens of papers from 2009 onwards linking ocean acidification from rising carbon dioxide to negative changes in fish behaviour, including numerous papers by JCU scientist Philip Munday and his PhD student Danielle Dixson.[45] Not only did Clark et al find that the research by Munday, Dixson and others could not be replicated, but they pointed to problems with the data and analysis that several experts indicated was possible fraud.

This followed another scandal involving another of Munday's PhD students, Oona Lönnstedt who was found to have committed fraud as a postdoctoral fellow at Uppsala University in Sweden. Attention was then focused on her work while at JCU, where she was a star graduate student, with 20 publications – outstanding for a graduate student.

Dixson and Lönnstedt had both been supervised by Munday at JCU. Timothy Clark had been at the AIMS in Townsville; Fredrik Jutfelt and Josefin Sundin had witnessed Lönnstedt's research in Sweden, so three of the authors of the *Nature* paper in 2020 had, along with others who had been at JCU, been physically close to research conducted by both Dixson and Lönnstedt. A long article in *Science* reported that Munday had written to Lönnstedt in June 2016 when she was under investigation in Sweden and made a remarkable statement that attests to a response to scientific criticism that is more Feyerabend than Popper, and shows just how undervalued falsification can be:

> It seems that Clark and Jutfelt are trying to make a career out of criticizing other people's work. I can only assume they don't have enough good ideas of their own to fill in their time ... Recently, I found out they have been "secretly" doing work on the behavioural effects of high CO_2 on coral reef fishes, presumably because they want to be critical of some aspects of our work.[46]

JCU stated that it had dismissed the case brought by the Clark group following the advice of an external investigator, but Clark et al drew wide praise. This included ecotoxicologist John Sumpter of Brunel University London, who was quoted as saying, "It is by far the best environmental science paper I have read for a long time".[47]

With both the JCU and Uppsala University cases, Lönnstedt's supervisors confessed to not having any direct knowledge of her conducting her experiments, despite being co-authors. That proved to be a grave error. Lönnstedt's 2012 experiments on Lizard Island would have required her to catch 86 zebra lionfish and 16 spotfin lionfish.[48] The Lizard Island Research Station had a protocol where all researchers must record their catch. A whistleblower reported to *Science* that the online record of fish collections showed that Lönnstedt caught only 12 zebra lionfish and three spotfin lionfish during her 2012 trip.[49]

After the Swedish case, JCU enquired into Dr Lönnstedt's research, with the Deputy Vice-Chancellor (Research and Innovation) writing to his Vice-Chancellor Sandra Harding on 28 March 2018, as required by JCU procedure, after a Swedish and a Canadian researcher each raised issues when their requests for Lönnstedt's data could not be met. An internal review drew attention to issues involving research ethics, data integrity and data availability. In January 2019, a JCU spokesman stated that an external panel had been "finalised" to investigate Lönnstedt's research, but the panel was not appointed until 12 December 2019, and did not report until June 2020 – more than two years after concerns were first raised. As Walter Starck observed, "One might be forgiven for wondering if JCU has dragged its heels in hope that the whole thing would blow over and be forgotten."[50]

By establishing an external review in response to the concerns raised by the DVC, JCU limited the scope of the enquiry. One of the papers that Clark et al found could not be replicated involved Lönnstedt, but that was not considered by the review panel. The review, nonetheless, found numerous problems with Lönnstedt's research. Research ethics approval was sought after research had commenced. Data had not been properly archived. There were discrepancies between the numbers of fish Lönnstedt's publications reported as having been used and those recorded at the Lizard Island Research Station. Despite all this, the panel found that there had been no deliberate malpractice or fraud. This was despite Lönnstedt's research practices and record-keeping appearing to be quite similar to those that got her into trouble in Sweden.

There was one remarkable statement in the panel's report:

There is no evidence to suggest that fish were not caught or experimental work not done during the initial period of intense fieldwork and laboratory work at Lizard Island in the spring/summer of 2010–2011, or in late 2012.[51]

The logical impossibility of proving a negative, that any evidence could establish that something did not happen, seems to have escaped the panel. The panel did find evidence of fieldwork started and/or conducted prior to the approved date of project fieldwork commencement, sloppiness (at best) in data recording that led to multiple inconsistencies in data, and inadequate archiving of data, but concluded that Dr Lönnstedt did not engage in research misconduct. It simply waved away the points raised by Enserink[52] and earlier by Ridd, which cited experts in visual recognition that several of the lionfish in the montage she produced were deliberately manipulated images of the same fish, by, for example, accepting the lame explanation that the montage had been prepared earlier when not meant to convey the size of the sample and then used for that purpose with insufficient care.

One might consider that the panel was rather incurious and that – eventually – it examined "issues" raised by the Deputy Vice-Chancellor rather than formal complaints, and that this had the effect of forestalling subsequent complaints, but that is not my focus here.

Rather, what the investigation shows is that Ridd was correct to raise criticisms of the lack of adequate QA on research on the GBR (including Dr Lönnstedt's fish), because the panel's report alone stands as an indictment that proves his case, because it concludes that there was sloppy, but not fraudulent, research. Add the work by Clark et al on the failure to replicate work coming out of JCU (published while the panel was deliberating, and including another paper involving Lönnstedt) and there are serious questions evident concerning QA about reef science at JCU

A personal observation: it seems that these several studies of the effects of elevated CO_2 on fish, often using the concentration "expected" in 2100, made no allowance for the possibility that the various fish species over the intervening 90-odd years might adapt physiologically, and possibly even genetically. The issue is highlighted by a brief description of the method in Ferrari et al: "Juvenile damselfish exposed to 440 (current day control), 550 or 700µatm CO_2 did not differ in their response ... However, fish exposed to 850µatm showed reduced antipredator responses ..."[53]

In other words, the fish only exhibited an effect when suddenly exposed to an almost double concentration of CO_2. In addition, Walter Starck pointed out the reduction in pH predicted for 2100 is frequently exceeded on shallow reef tops during low tide at night, when photosynthesis has ceased, so that CO_2 is not being consumed and the animal organisms continue to produce it.[54]

It should be noted that *all* research that refers to "ocean acidification" should be regarded with a suspicion that it has a "value slope" and seeks to build alarm over climate change. It is settled science that sea water has a pH of about 8.1, and is a buffered solution that resists change. Note also that the pH scale is logarithmic, so that 8.0 is ten times more alkaline than 7.0 (neutral). It is highly unlikely that the pH of the oceans will be reduced below 7.0, but "acidification" sounds much scarier than "neutralisation".

By attempting to silence Ridd, JCU was suppressing an important critical view of the quality of research on the GBR, and those close to poor science are often best placed to expose it. Ridd's criticisms were, of course, a threat to the standing of the CECRS and AIMS, both of which were important to JCU. The Turnbull government allocated $444 million three years after Ridd's criticism of GBR science, and one assumes that they did so thinking that the science was sound. A notable case of scientific malpractice in Australia demonstrates that institutions are likely to protect themselves, rather than the integrity of science. But insiders can be crucial to exposing malpractice.

A different case: Michael Briggs

A brief study of a notorious case of scientific fraud reveals much about the way universities can fail to expose scientific misconduct, and why those within them are often best placed to blow the whistle on malpractice. The case involves Michael Briggs, who was a star researcher at Deakin University, bringing welcome research grant riches to a newly formed university in the late 1970s. There had been critics of Briggs from the outset of his time at Deakin, but the amount of industrial funding he attracted meant that he was difficult to challenge. Vice-Chancellor Fred Jevons put questions from anonymous scientists to Briggs but the university decided not to proceed further.[55] Briggs, funded by a pharmaceutical company, published, *inter alia*, papers such as "Progestogens and mammary tumours in the beagle bitch".[56] The problem was, nobody at Deakin had seen a beagle. As Brian Deer put it so neatly in a retrospective analysis, "There are a few things you might need for an experiment involving beagles and the side effects of contraceptive pills. Animal research ethics aside, beagles might be a good start."[57]

Briggs was eventually exposed thanks to the tenacious efforts of a local medical practitioner, Dr Jim Rossiter, who saw problems with Briggs's research and pressed the case against him, despite Briggs taking legal action and using a procedural point to block an investigation by the university. Martin noted that "for his pains, Rossiter received hundreds of threatening phone calls".[58] The university administration, in other words, went to water in the face of legal threats, but the damage to the reputation of the university was limited, belatedly, by Dr Rossiter – who, as it happened, was a member of the Deakin University Council.

The lesson from the Briggs case is that those inside a university are often best placed to raise the alarm on problems with the research of their colleagues, but there are many institutional factors that make them unlikely to do so. As Martin put it, "All this suggests that the priority is on limiting not fraud but damage to the reputations of the institutions concerned".[59] The conduct of JCU certainly bears this out. When Ridd raised criticisms of the standard of QA surrounding reef science in its lucrative CECRS, it went after the whistleblower rather than investigate his claims, thus prioritising protecting the institution. Unfortunately, the High Court ruled that Peter Ridd should have remained silent and accepted an improper censure so that a matter of considerable public importance should be suppressed, rather than finding in favour of free speech.

Government-funded science

In addition to normative beliefs, the other source of a value slope is money, and much of it today comes from governments that have been generous in the extreme in funding attempts, effectively, to prevent the reef from changing – indeed, tilting at windmills by attempting to stop the coral from engaging in its usual adaptation response. The pernicious effect of this relationship was the basis of a warning given in 1961 by President Eisenhower in his farewell address. That address is remembered more for his warning of the "Military-Industrial Complex", but his wise words about the pernicious effect of government funding on the conduct of science – often forgotten – are worth quoting at length. Eisenhower stated:

Today, the solitary inventor, tinkering in his shop, has been overshadowed by task forces of scientists in laboratories and testing fields. In the same fashion, the free university, historically the fountainhead of free ideas and scientific discovery, has experienced a revolution in the conduct of research. Partly because of the huge costs involved, a government contract becomes virtually a substitute for intellectual curiosity. For every old blackboard there are now hundreds of new electronic computers.

The prospect of domination of the nation's scholars by Federal employment, project allocations, and the power of money is ever present and is gravely to be regarded.

Yet, in holding scientific research and discovery in respect, as we should, we must also be alert to the equal and opposite danger that public policy could itself become the captive of a scientific-technological elite.[60]

C.P. Snow put it succinctly when he suggested that scientists should be on tap, not on top, but the demands that we "follow The Science" evident in both the climate debate and the recent Covid-19 pandemic show that there are plenty of scientists who are only too happy to attempt to impose their will on democratic governance. And while the alarmist Covid modelling that led to actions that were devastating in their impact on societies, economies, and psychology, that underlying climate science is still accepted by policy makers – even though the worst projections of doom are driven by the discredited Representative Concentration Pathway 8.5, a greenhouse gas concentration trajectory so unrealistic that even some climate modellers have disavowed it.[61] It still features prominently in the latest IPCC assessment reports.

Apart from the point that the notion there is something called "The Science" (note the capitalisation) is a nonsense, science cannot tell us what to do. It can serve as an important basis for public policy, but policy makers must also consider costs (economic and social), trade-offs, social and environmental impacts, and so on. Climate science cannot answer basic questions, such was whether we should seek to mitigate or adapt, or what balance we might choose between both.

The National Coral Bleaching Taskforce, established in about 2016 and designed to co-ordinate research efforts among Australia's marine science community in the event of a mass bleaching event in Australia, is especially problematic, as it narrows fundamentally the range of viewpoints available to inform the policy discourse. It draws together the CECRS, AIMS, CSIRO, Great Barrier Reef Marine Park Authority (GBRMPA), JCU, NOAA, The University of Queensland, University of Sydney, University of Western Australia, and WA Department of Parks and Wildlife. The CECRS itself draws together many of these institutions: JCU, AIMS, GBRMPA, The University of Queensland, and the University of Western Australia.

This taskforce is problematic because, like the IPCC, it is an attempt to create a monopoly on scientific advice that might be given to governments. The crucial question is: from where might critical views that differ from those developed by the taskforce come? In other words, where will be the external review that will guard against groupthink? This amounts to an exacerbation of Eisenhower's warning, and the questions over GBR science I have outlined above simply reinforce Ridd's view that such QA is sorely needed.

Alarmism over the reef has proven profitable but appears to have run its course. A paper published in *Nature Ecology & Evolution* in 2021 (with Terry Hughes as a co-author) concluded that, "while local depletions pose imminent threats that can have ecologically devastating impacts to coral reefs, the global extinction risk of most coral species is lower than previously estimated".[62]

There must be open contestation in both the natural and social sciences as the basis for policy-making. There is a reason why Karl Popper was a liberal in his political philosophy, arguing as he did that knowledge advances through disagreement. Autocracies are not known for the quality of their policy decisions. Lysenkoism and Soviet autocracy were mutually dependent. As Richard Feynman put it, science is a belief in the ignorance of experts.

Any institution, be it a government agency or a university, that tries to quash the voices of those who attempt to subject experts to critical scrutiny have dishonoured science. They are not in scientific Kansas anymore.

A cascade of injustice

The ever-changing reef was not a cause for concern until scientists first noticed crown-of-thorns starfish and then later coral bleaching – though both had certainly occurred previously. Only with the ascendancy of the view of "the delicate, harmonious balance of nature" did the changes in the reef become a cause for its likely demise, initially from the pressures of tourism. Then, as the 1990s progressed, and El Niño hit, climate change became a useful, dominant cause. The meme that the reef is dying and that climate change is the cause can be understood by reference to the concept of an "availability cascade", a self-reinforcing cycle that explains the development of a collective belief in such a phenomenon.

A number of possibly unrelated phenomena (cyclones, rising sea levels, ocean acidification, periodic bleaching, changes in salinity) with complex causes are explained by one, simple, easily understood cause. The explanation quickly becomes accepted because of its very simplicity and by its apparent insightfulness. Then follows a social chain reaction. Individuals adopt the insight that we are killing the reef through catastrophic anthropogenic climate change because others within their social network have adopted it. The availability of the explanation cascades because of social phenomena. As Kuran and Sunstein put it:

> Individuals endorse the perception partly by learning from the apparent beliefs of others and partly by distorting their public responses in the interest of maintaining social acceptance. Availability entrepreneurs – activists who manipulate the content of public discourse – strive to trigger availability cascades likely to advance their agendas.[63]

Insistence on open, contested science is the only counter to this form of groupthink, and this is what first JCU and then the High Court have prevented. Many universities have clauses in their enterprise agreements similar to that used to silence Ridd; there is an urgent need for them to discard these and commit to the principles of academic freedom advanced by Flynn.[64] The injustice is not just to Ridd (though that is serious enough), but to the conduct of science, especially as it informs public policy – and thus to the public at large.

The public has a right to expect universities to be cathedrals of knowledge, but nobody expects the Roman Inquisition.

Acknowlegement

I thank Peter Ridd, Tim Clark and Martin Frické for their comments on an earlier version of this paper. Any errors or omissions are, of course, mine.

1   J Flynn, *What is Intelligence? Beyond the Flynn Effect* (Cambridge University Press, 2007).

2   JPA Ioannidis, 'Why Most Published Research Findings Are False' (2005) 2(8) *PLoS Medicine*, 696–70.

3   AJ Ayer, *Language, Truth and Logic* (2nd ed. Victor Gollancz, 1946).

4   *Daubert v. Merrel Dow Pharmaceuticals, Inc.*, 509 US 579 (1993); 43 F 3d 1311 (9th Cir. 1995).

5   See K Popper, *The Logic of Scientific Discovery*, (Routledge, 2005), and K Popper, *Conjectures and Refutations: The Growth of Scientific Knowledge* (Routledge, 2014).

6   TS Kuhn, *The Structure of Scientific Revolutions* (University of Chicago Press, 1962).

7   P Feyerabend, *Against Method: Outline of an Anarchistic Theory of Knowledge* (New Left Books, 1975).

8   S Murudkar, 'Top 10 journals to publish your negative results', (2021) Enago Academy. <https://www.enago.com/academy/top-10-journals-publish-negative-results/>.

9   O Hoegh-Guldberg 'Climate change, coral bleaching and the future of the world's coral reefs' (1999) 50(8) *Marine and Freshwater Research* 839-866.

10 See for instance HS Sweatman, S Delean, and C Syms, 'Assessing loss of coral cover on Australia's Great Barrier Reef over two decades, with implications for longer term-trends' (2011) 30 *Coral Reefs* 521–531; and TP Hughes, DR Bellwood, AH Baird, J Brodie, JF Bruno, JM Pandolfi, 'Shifting base-lines, declining coral cover, and the erosion of reef resilience. Comment on Sweatman et al.' (2011) 30(3) *Coral Reefs* 653-660.

11   T Blair, 'Eternal Life and Death of Our Rare Roast Reef',
      Daily Telegraph, 11 June 2017 (accessed online) <https://www.
      dailytelegraph.com.au/blogs/tim-blair/eternal-life-and-death-of-our-
      rare-roast-reef/news-story/4631e7f45c1602afaa46bbe2b6f4e365#>.

12   S Choukroun, PV Ridd, R Brinkman, and LI McKinna, 'On the
      surface circulation in the western Coral Sea and residence times
      in the Great Barrier Reef' (2010) 115(C6) *Journal of Geophysical
      Research: Oceans.*

13   A Kellow, *Science and Public Policy: The Virtuous Corruption of Virtual
      Environmental Science* (Edward Elgar Publishing 2007).

14   I Boal, 'A flow of monsters: luddism and virtual technologies' in J
      Brook and I Boal (eds), *Resisting the Virtual Life: The Culture and
      Politics of Information* (City Lights, 1995) 3-15.

15   B Yandle, 'Bootleggers and Baptists-the education of a regulatory
      economist' (1983) 7 *Regulation*, 12–16.

16   T Fielding, 'Expedition to the Great Barrier Reef 1928–29 Parts
      1–5' (2018) *JCU Library News* <https://jculibrarynews.blogspot.
      com/2018/08/expedition-to-great-barrier-reef-1928.html>.

17   See, for example, DT Suzuki, and A McConnell, *The Sacred Balance:
      Rediscovering Our Place in Nature* (Allen & Unwin, 1997).

18   DJ Frederick, 'Great Barrier Reef Awash with Horror Stories:
      Australia: Pollution, oil spills, overfishing and more than a million
      tourists a year threaten the coral and furrow the brows of scientists
      and environmentalists.' *Los Angeles Times*, 6 March 1994 (accessed
      online) <https://www.latimes.com/archives/la-xpm-1994-03-06-mn-
      30613-story.html>.

19   R Jacobsen, 'Obituary: Great Barrier Reef (25 Million BC-
      ...)', *Outside*, 11 October 2016 (accessed online) <https://www.
      outsideonline.com/outdoor-adventure/environment/obituary-great-
      barrier-reef-25-million-bc-2016/>.

20   O Milman, 'The Great Barrier Reef is under severe stress – but not
      dead yet', *The Guardian*, 14 October 2016 (access online) <https://
      www.theguardian.com/us-news/2016/oct/14/great-barrier-reef-
      severe-stress-not-dead-yet>.

21   C D'Angelo, 'Great Barrier Reef Obituary Goes Viral, To The
     Horror Of Scientists', *Huffington Post*, 14 October 2016 (accessed
     online) <https://www.huffpost.com/entry/scientists-take-on-great-
     barrier-reef-obituary_n_57fff8f1e4b0162c043b068f>.

22   B Tobin, 'How the Great Barrier Reef was formed. 20,000 years ago
     to present – a concise treatise' (2003) <https://www.aims.gov.au/docs/
     projectnet/how-the-gbr-was-formed.html>.

23   TF Goreau, 'Mass expulsion of zooxanthellae from Jamaican
     reef communities after Hurricane Flora' (1964) 145(3630) *Science*
     383–386.

24   TP Hughes, 'Catastrophes, phase shifts, and large-scale degradation
     of a Caribbean coral reef.' (1994) 265(5178) *Science* 1547, 1549.

25   O Hoegh-Guldberg, 'Climate change, coral bleaching and the
     future of the world's coral reefs' (1999) 50(8) *Marine and Freshwater
     Research* 839-866.

26   NA Kamenos, and SJ Hennige, 'Reconstructing four centuries of
     temperature-induced coral bleaching on the Great Barrier Reef'
     (2018) 5 *Frontiers in Marine Science* 283.

27   O Hoegh-Guldberg, WJ Skirving, JM Lough, C Liu, ME Mann,
     S Donner, CM Eakin, et al, 'Commentary: reconstructing four
     centuries of temperature-induced coral bleaching on the Great
     Barrier Reef' (2019) 6 *Frontiers in Marine Science* 86.

28   A Kellow, 'Climate science and policy-based evidence' in Jennifer
     Marohasy (ed) *Climate Change: The Facts* 2020 (IPA, 2021).

29   CM Yonge, 'Final report on the Great Barrier Reef Expedition'
     (1929) 124(3131) *Nature* 694-697.

30   T Fielding, 'Expedition to the Great Barrier Reef 1928–29 Parts
     1–5' (2018) *JCU Library News* <https://jculibrarynews.blogspot.
     com/2018/08/expedition-to-great-barrier-reef-1928.html>.

31   TF Goreau, 'Mass expulsion of zooxanthellae from Jamaican reef
     communities after Hurricane Flora' (1964) 145(3630) *Science* 383–386.

32   O Hoegh-Guldberg, 'Climate change, coral bleaching and the
     future of the world's coral reefs' (1999) 50(8) *Marine and Freshwater
     Research* 839-866.

33   O Hoegh-Guldberg, 'Climate change, coral bleaching and the future of the world's coral reefs' (1999) 50(8) *Marine and Freshwater Research* 839-866.

34   P Larcombe and P Ridd, 'The need for a formalised system of Quality Control for environmental policy-science' (2018) 126 *Marine Pollution Bulletin* 449-461.

35   B Schaffelke, K Fabricius, F Kroon, J Brodie, G De'ath, R Shaw, D Tarte, M Warne, and P Thorburn, 'Support for improved quality control but misplaced criticism of GBR science. Reply to viewpoint "The need for a formalised system of Quality Control for environmental policy-science" by P Larcombe and P Ridd in (2018) 126 *Marine Pollution Bulletin* 449–461', 129(1) *Marine Pollution Bulletin* 357, 358.

36   SE Koonin, *Unsettled: What Climate Science Tells Us, What It Doesn't, and Why It Matters* (BenBella Books 2021).

37   EJ Calabrese, and LA Baldwin, 'Toxicology rethinks its central belief' (2003) 421(6924) *Nature* 691-692.

38   M Grubb, 'We're climate researchers and our work was turned into fake news' *The Conversation* (online 26 January 2018) <https://theconversation.com/were-climate-researchers-and-our- work-was-turned-into-fake-news-89999>.

39   WWF, 'European economists and WWF call for stronger EU carbon market' (online 9 November 2006) <https://wwf.panda.org/wwf_news/?85860/European-economists-and-WWF-call-for-stronger-EU-carbon-market>.

40   A Auliciems, and I Burton, 'Trends in smoke concentrations before and after the Clean Air Act of 1956' (1973) 7 *Atmospheric Environment* 1063–70; HA Scarrow, 'The impact of British domestic air pollution legislation' (1972) 2 *British Journal of Political of Science* 261–82.

41   O Hoegh-Guldberg, 'Climate change, coral bleaching and the future of the world's coral reefs' (1999) 50(8) *Marine and Freshwater Research* 839-866.

42   P Larcombe and P Ridd, 'The need for a formalised system of Quality Control for environmental policy-science' (2018) 126 *Marine Pollution Bulletin* 449-461.

43   B Schaffelke, K Fabricius, F Kroon, J Brodie, G De'ath, R Shaw, D Tarte, M Warne, and P Thorburn, 'Support for improved quality control but misplaced criticism of GBR science. Reply to viewpoint "The need for a formalised system of Quality Control for environmental policy-science" by P Larcombe and P Ridd in (2018) 126 *Marine Pollution Bulletin* 449–461', 129(1) *Marine Pollution Bulletin* 357–363.

44   M Enserink, 'Fishy business' (2017) 355(6331) *Science* 1254–1257; M Enserink, 'Swedish plastics study fabricated, panel finds' (2017) 358(6369) *Science* 1367.

45   TD Clark, GD Raby, DG Roche, SA Binning, B Speers-Roesch, F Jutfelt, and J Sundin, 'Ocean acidification does not impair the behaviour of coral reef fishes' (2020) 577(7790) *Nature* 370–375.

46   M Enserink, 'Sea of Doubts' (2021) 372(6542) *Science* 560–565.

47   M Enserink, 'Sea of Doubts' (2021) 372(6542) *Science* 560–565.

48   OM Lönnstedt, MC Ferrari, and DP Chivers, 'Lionfish predators use flared fin displays to initiate cooperative hunting' (2014) 10(6) *Biology letters*.

49   M Enserink, 'Duplicated images point to fraud in fish study, critics say' (2019) 366(6461) *Science* 20–21.

50   W Starck, 'The Tip of a JCU's Junk Science Iceberg', *Quadrant*, 5 February 2020 (accessed online). <https://quadrant.org.au/opinion/doomed-planet/2020/02/the-tip-of-a-jcus-junk-science-iceberg/>.

51   James Cook University Independent External Research Misconduct Inquiry Panel, *Report of the Independent External Research Misconduct Inquiry: Dr Oona Lönndstedt* (2020).

52   M Enserink, 'Duplicated images point to fraud in fish study, critics say' (2019) 366(6461) *Science* 20–21.

53 MC Ferrari, MI McCormick, PL Munday, MG Meekan, DL Dixson, O Lönnstedt, and DP Chivers, 'Effects of ocean acidification on visual risk assessment in coral reef fishes' (2012) 26(3) *Functional Ecology* 553-558.

54 W Starck, 'The Tip of a JCU's Junk Science Iceberg', *Quadrant*, 5 February 2020 (accessed online). <https://quadrant.org.au/opinion/doomed-planet/2020/02/the-tip-of-a-jcus-junk-science-iceberg/>.

55 B Martin, 'Scientific fraud and the power structure of science' (1992) 10(1) *Prometheus* 83–98.

56 MH Briggs, 'Progestogens and mammary tumours in the beagle bitch' (1980) 28(2) *Research in veterinary science* 199–202.

57 B Deer, 'Exposed: the bogus work of Professor Briggs', *The Sunday Times*, 28 September 1986 (accessed online) <https://briandeer.com/michael-briggs-1.htm>.

58 B Martin, 'Scientific fraud and the power structure of science' (1992) 10(1) *Prometheus* 83, 93.

59 Ibid.

60 DD Eisenhower, Farewell Address (1961) (online) <https://www.archives.gov/milestone-documents/president-dwight-d-eisenhowers-farewell-address>.

61 Z Hausfather, and GP Peters, 'Emissions – the "business as usual" story is misleading' (2020) *Nature* 618-620; MG Burgess, J Ritchie, J Shapland, and R Pielke, 'IPCC baseline scenarios have over-projected CO_2 emissions and economic growth' (2020) 16(1) *Environmental Research Letters*.

62 A Dietzel, M Bode, SR Connolly, and TP Hughes, 'The population sizes and global extinction risk of reef-building coral species at biogeographic scales' (2021) 5(5) *Nature Ecology & Evolution* 663–669.

63 T Kuran, and CR Sunstein, 'Availability cascades and risk regulation' (1998) 51 *Stan. L. Rev.* 683–768.

64 JR Flynn, *A Book too Risky to Publish: Free Speech and Universities* (Academica Press, 2020).

Appendix: Extracts of key legal documents

James Cook University Enterprise Agreement 2013-2016

---

13. Code of Conduct

13.1. The parties agree that the Code of Conduct will only be changed following consultation with the JCC.

13.2. JCU is committed to achieving and maintaining the highest standards of ethical conduct and through the Code of Conduct will ensure that staff:

- Seek excellence as a part of a learning community;
- Act with integrity;
- Behave with respect for others; and
- Embrace sustainability and social responsibility.

13.3. The parties note that the Code of Conduct is not intended to detract from Clause 14, *Intellectual Freedom*.

14. Intellectual Freedom

14.1. JCU is committed to act in a manner consistent with the protection and promotion of intellectual freedom within the University and in accordance with JCU's Code of Conduct.

14.2. freedom includes the rights of staff to:
- Pursue critical and open inquiry;

- Participate in public debate and express opinions about issues and ideas related to their respective fields of competence;
- Express opinions about the operations of JCU and higher education policy more generally;
- Be eligible to participate in established decision making structures and processes within JCU, subject to established selection procedures and criteria;
- Participate in professional and representative bodies, including unions and other representative bodies.

14.3. All staff have the right to express unpopular or controversial views. However, this comes with a responsibility to respect the rights of others and they do not have the right to harass, vilify, bully or intimidate those who disagree with their views. These rights are linked to the responsibilities of staff to support JCU as a place independent learning and thought where ideas may be put forward and opinion expressed freely.

14.4. JCU acknowledges the rights of staff to express disagreement with University decisions and with the processes used to make those decisions. Staff should seek to raise their concerns through applicable processes and give reasonable opportunity for such processes to be followed.

54. Misconduct/Serious Misconduct

54.1. General Principles

54.1.1 The principles of procedural fairness and natural justice will be applied to all Misconduct and Serious Misconduct processes outlined in this clause.

54.1.2 Matters involving underperformance are not considered Misconduct and are dealt with separately under Clause 42, Managing Underperformance.

54.1.3 Staff may choose to be represented in all/any meetings or discussions under this Clause 54 as provided for in Clause 11, Staff Support and Representation.

54.1.4 In the event of allegations of Serious Misconduct, the parties acknowledge that JCU may have an obligation to refer the conduct to the Crime and Misconduct Commission. The parties acknowledge that such referral may impact on the timeframes and ability for JCU to respond and investigate matters under this clause.

54.1.5 The confidentiality of all parties involved in the management of Misconduct and Serious Misconduct processes will be respected and all information gathered and recorded will remain confidential, subject to JCU's obligations:

a) to discharge its responsibilities under an Act or University policy;

b) for a proceeding in a court or tribunal; or

c) unless the person to whom the confidential information relates, consents in writing to the disclosure of the information or record; or if no consent is obtainable and such disclosure is unlikely to harm the interests of the person affected; or

d) unless the information is already in the public domain.

James Cook University Staff Code of Conduct (28 April 2016)

———

Intent

The Code of Conduct establishes a standard by which we conduct ourselves towards others and perform our professional duties on behalf of the University. Its aim is to help us to aspire to the highest standards of ethical conduct. The Code must be read in conjunction with the Explanatory Statement for the Code of Conduct which provides further detail regarding the required standards of conduct.

Scope

The Code of Conduct applies to all staff of James Cook University while acting in their official capacity.

Definitions

Public comment – includes public speaking engagements, comments on radio and television; and expressing views in letters to the newspapers or in books, journals or notices, or where it might be expected that the publication or circulation of the comment will spread to the community at large.

Staff – for the purposes of this Code, means ongoing, fixed-term and casual staff, including senior management, executive, academic, professional and technical, visiting and adjunct staff, volunteers and conjoint appointments.

Policy

The [*Public Sector Ethics Act 1994* (Qld)] outlines four fundamental ethical principles which are fundamental to good public administration:

- integrity and impartiality,
- promoting the public good,
- commitment to the system of government, and
- accountability and transparency.

These ethical principles form the basis of the obligations outlined in this Code of Conduct and the associated Explanatory Statement.

In giving expression to the Act, the University has developed the Code of Conduct around four principles which will act to guide the actions of staff. These principles are outlined below.

Principle 1: Seek excellence as part of a learning community

This principle aligns with the first ethical principle of the Act – 'integrity and impartiality', and the second ethical principle of the Act – 'promoting the public good'.

In our conduct, we will:

- value academic freedom, and enquire, examine, criticise and challenge in the collegial and academic spirit of the search for knowledge, understanding and truth;
- behave with intellectual honesty;
- have the right to make public comment in a professional, expert or individual capacity, provided that we do not represent our opinions as those of the University unless authorised to do so;
- have the right to freedom of expression, provided that our speech is lawful and respects the rights of others;

Principle 2: Act with integrity

This principle aligns with the first ethical principle of the Act – 'integrity and impartiality', with the third ethical principle – 'commitment to the system of government', and with the fourth ethical principle – 'accountability and transparency'.

In our conduct, we will:

- maintain appropriate confidentiality regarding University business;
- act with authenticity, sincerity and truthfulness;
- engage in genuine dialogue with other staff, students and stakeholders through transparent, open and honest communication and consultation;
- ensure that ethical governance structures and systems are established and maintained;
- behave in a way that upholds the integrity and good reputation of the University;
- take responsibility for our mistakes, work to rectify problems as soon as possible, and ensure that those who have admitted mistakes are treated with fairness and dignity;
- comply with any lawful and reasonable direction given by someone who has authority to give that direction;
- make well-considered decisions, and provide reasons for these decisions where required, especially where they may have an adverse effect on people;
- act within the limits of our authority;
- disclose wrongdoing and protect those who make a disclosure;

Principle 3: Behave with respect for others

This principle aligns with the first ethical principle of the Act – 'integrity and impartiality'.
In our conduct, we will:

- treat fellow staff members, students and members of the public with honesty, respect and courtesy, and have regard for the dignity and needs of others;
- act to ensure equity, fairness and natural justice is afforded to all;
- seek to resolve disputes in a fair and timely manner;
- investigate any complaints that have been lodged against staff or students in a consistent, prompt, fair and timely manner;
- avoid and not accept behaviours which are unwelcome, discriminatory, intimidatory or abusive;
- stand up for the rights of others;

Compliance with the Code of Conduct and associated Explanatory Statement

- The University is committed to providing staff with access to education and training in relation to the requirements of this Code and the associated Explanatory Statement for the Code of Conduct.
- Where uncertain about the Code's application or interpretation, staff should consult with their Director/College Dean or higher authority if appropriate.
- Failure to comply with the Code may lead to disciplinary action, and in serious cases may lead to termination of employment and/or criminal prosecution.

Contributors

Peter Ridd

Peter Ridd is a former professor and Head of Physics (2009-2016) at James Cook University (Townsville). He has published more than 100 papers in international science journals and supervised many successful PhD students. His most recent book is *Reef Heresy? Science, Research and the Great Barrier Reef.*

Morgan Begg

Morgan Begg is the Director of Research at the Institute of Public Affairs. Morgan joined the IPA in 2014 to advance a major report into The State of Fundamental Legal Rights in Australia. Since then, Morgan has also written several research papers, opinion articles, *IPA Review* essays and submissions to parliamentary inquiries, on a variety of topics.

Chris Merritt

Chris Merritt is a weekly columnist at *The Australian* newspaper and Vice President of the Rule of Law Education Centre. Chris was the foremost commentator on rule of law issues in Australia as editor of the legal affairs section of *The Australian* from 2005 until 2020.

James Allen
James Allen is Garrick Professor of Law at the University of Queensland. He has been published widely in the areas of legal philosophy, constitutional law. James' latest book is *The Age of Foolishness: A Doubter's Guide to Constitutionalism in a Modern Democracy.*

Aynsley Kellow
Aynsley Kellow holds a PhD in political studies from the University of Otago and is currently an Emeritus Professor at the University of Tasmania where he taught for over 20 years. He was an expert reviewer for the IPCC's Fourth Assessment Report.

www.ingramcontent.com/pod-product-compliance
Lightning Source LLC
Chambersburg PA
CBHW070356200326
41518CB00012B/2249

* 9 7 8 1 9 2 3 2 2 4 4 0 7 *